LET US RISE UP AND BUILD

*Transforming Principles
Exemplified in the
Life and Ministry of Nehemiah*

By

Dr. Ronald L. Bernier

© **Copyright 2004 – Dr. Ronald L. Bernier**
All rights reserved. This book is protected under the copyright laws of the United States of America. This book may not be copied or reprinted for commercial gain or profit. The use of short quotations or occasional page copying for personal or group study is permitted and encouraged. Permission will be granted upon request. Unless otherwise identified, Scripture quotations are from the New King James Version of the Bible.

Published by **Vision Publishing.**
Ramona, California
www.vision.edu

ISBN 1-931178-71-2

FOR INFORMATION ON ORDERING PLEASE CONTACT:

MASTER BUILDER MINISTRIES, INC.
397 Bay Street
Fall River, MA 02724
508-730-1735
or

Vision Publishing
1-800-9VISION

PRINTED IN THE UNITED STATES OF AMERICA

CONTENTS

FOREWORD 5
INTRODUCTION 7
CHAPTER 1 9
OVERCOMING INDIFFERENCE 9
CHAPTER 2 17
COMMITTING TO ACTION 17
CHAPTER 3 25
BUILDING WITH A TEAM 25
CHAPTER 4 37
LEADING DESPITE OPPOSITION 37
CHAPTER 5 45
A THREAT FROM WITHIN 45
CHAPTER 6 53
CONFRONTING PERSONAL ATTACKS 53
CHAPTER 7 61
BROADING COMMUNITY INFLUENCE 61
CHAPTER 8 71
PEOPLE OF THE BOOK 71

CHAPTER 9	77
REMEMBERING OUR HERITAGE	77
CHAPTER 10	87
BUILDING THROUGH COVENANT	87
CHAPTER 11	93
MODELING PROPER GOVERNMENT	93
CHAPTER 12	107
JOYFUL CELEBRATION	107
CHAPTER 13	117
LIFELONG SERVANT LEADERSHIP	117
BIBLIOGRAPHY	127

FOREWORD

Not every writer has the ability to express his or her heart in what they expound. Not every pastor can express his or her true desire to see God's people become all He intended. Not all spiritual leaders have sufficient self-consciousness nor spiritual sensitivity to express the Fathers heart for the benefit of others. In this book and with this Pastor and author, we find a rare exception.

Dr. Ronald Bernier has written a wonderful treatise on church life, its functions and dysfunctions, despair and recovery, rooted in biblical revelation. Using the book of Nehemiah and keen analysis and synthesis, Pastor Bernier presents eternal truths in practical, useable format.

It has been a delight and challenge to read this well thought, well written commentary on one of the bibles great leaders, made contemporary for our edification.

Dr. Stan E. DeKoven, President
Vision Christian University

INTRODUCTION

Where in Scripture do we see evidence that the body of Christ really can be effective in holistic ministry in the city? To answer this question, we must first ask: "What are the marks of truly effective urban ministry?"

1. Are the systems of a city being confronted and offered real potential for change?

2. Are the poor and exploited of the city provided the vehicles by which they can bring about change in their situation?

3. Are the middle class and the powerful given opportunity to join in common cause with the poor to confront the systems of the city and seek their transformation?

4. Is there a spiritual transformation that is going on in that city, or are the changes only social? Are both the lives of that city's poor and of its powerful being changed by God?

Therefore we must ask ourselves: "In Scripture, is there any example of an urban ministry which exhibits these four marks of truly effective ministry? There are examples in Scripture of many ministries that significantly address their cities, but one example of a city ministry stands head and shoulders above all others.

This ministry confronted the city's systems and saw significant transformation occur. This ministry organized the people of that city – both its poor and its powerful – to reverse the destructive directions of that city. A result of this ministry was a profound spiritual transformation, not only of the city itself, but also of an overwhelming majority of its people. This ministry of presence, prayer, practice, and proclamation exposed the lies of the powers that would have exploited that city, and it engaged the people in creating for themselves a new vision of what it meant for them to be "the city of God." This vision was so profound that it altered for all time the self-understanding and mission directions of the Jewish people.

The ministry was that of Nehemiah. The time was 445-433 B.C. The city was Jerusalem. The memoirs of Nehemiah's ministry, which became the Old Testament Book of Nehemiah, provide us with the best textbook has ever been written on how to undertake and transform urban ministry successfully. Let's examine that textbook to discover how to do ministry God's way!

CHAPTER 1
OVERCOMING INDIFFERENCE

Nehemiah 1:1-4 (NKJV)
The words of Nehemiah the son of Hachaliah. It came to pass in the month of Chislev, in the twentieth year, as I was in Shushan the citadel, [2] that Hanani one of my brethren came with men from Judah; and I asked them concerning the Jews who had escaped, who had survived the captivity, and concerning Jerusalem. [3] And they said to me, "The survivors who are left from the captivity in the province are there in great distress and reproach. The wall of Jerusalem is also broken down, and its gates are burned with fire."
[4] So it was, when I heard these words, that I sat down and wept, and mourned for many days; I was fasting and praying before the God of heaven.

Thus begins the book of Nehemiah. It begins with relatives of a man named Nehemiah coming to the capital of the Persian Empire, Susa, to visit him and so share with him the sad news that the once glorious Jerusalem had, since the Babylonian exile, eroded into a destitute and forsaken city. Who Nehemiah was and why he was in the Persian capital is not revealed until later in the story.

Nehemiah, upon hearing the sad news, dissolves into tears. His grief is not a short grief. He tells us, "that I sat down and wept, and mourned *for many* days; I was fasting and praying before the God of heaven." Commentators wonder about this strong reaction to the situation in Judah. Did Nehemiah actually know about the broken walls and the distressed society? Babylon had destroyed the walls in 587 B.C., 142 years before Hanani's report.

Why did Nehemiah react so profoundly? Was there a subsequent destruction of the walls after Ezra began His work (Ezra 4:7-23)? Perhaps Nehemiah heard old news from his Judean relatives, yet, for some reason, this time his heart was deeply moved by what he had known for years.

Was God preparing Nehemiah for service by opening his heart in a new way? Nehemiah allowed his heart to be broken with the things that break the heart of God. He did not try to avoid the pain nor dismiss his grief as he went about his daily tasks in Susa. Instead, he gave himself permission to experience that pain and to feel it to the very core of his being. Nehemiah understood grief and saw that its exploration is often the way people discover their vocations – for God always calls us to address a particular pain experienced in the world.

According to the editor of *American Opinion* who quotes the statement that William Schlamm has said to be the epitaph of our society "This civilization died because it didn't want to be bothered." The worst sin that we can commit against our fellow creatures is not to hate them, but to be indifferent towards them: that's the essence of inhumanity.

The parable of the Good Samaritan (Luke 10:25-37) addresses this issue. It rebukes all those who fold their arms complacently smile benignly, and say somewhat sarcastically, "Ask me if I care!" Nehemiah was a person who cared. He cared about the traditions of the past, the needs of the present, and the hopes for the future. He cared about his heritage, his ancestral city, and the glory of God.

One way Nehemiah demonstrated that he cared was to ask about the condition of Jerusalem. In response, he was given a dire report with two parts. First, the survivors, the remnant, that portion of Israel with whom the future was to lay, faced desperate economic times (Neh. 5:2-5). As a result, many people had been forced to sell themselves or their children into slavery. Leaders who later would be so ready to challenge Nehemiah (Neh. 2:19; 4:2-3) held pathetic little Judah in reproach.

The second aspect of the dire report concerned the "wall of Jerusalem". It was broken down and its gates are burned with fire" (vs. 3). Some people prefer not to know what's going on, because information might bring obligation. We ask people how they are doing – but don't really want to know. Francis Schaffer said that all this generation wants is affluence and personal peace. When we truly care about people, we want the facts no matter how painful they might be. Facts do not cease to exist because they are ignored.

For Nehemiah the word became a turning point in his life. Like large doors – great life-changing events can swing on very small hinges. It was just another day when Moses went out to care for his sheep, but on that day he heard the Lord's call and became a prophet (Exodus 3). It was an ordinary day when David was called home from shepherding his flock, but on that day, he was anointed king (1 Sam. 16). It was an ordinary day when Peter, Andrew, James and John were mending their nets after a night of failure, but that was the day Jesus called them to be fishers of men (Luke 5:1-11). We never know what God has in store, even common place conversations with a friend or relative, so, we keep our hearts open to God's providential leading.

A second way Nehemiah demonstrated that he cared was to weep (Neh. 1:4). What makes people laugh or weep is often an indication of character. People who laugh at others' mistakes or misfortunes, or who weep over trivial personal disappointments, are lacking either in culture or character, and possibly both. Sometimes weeping is a sign of weakness; but with Nehemiah, it was a sign of strength, as it was with Jeremiah (Jer. 9:1), Paul (Acts 20:19) and the Lord Jesus (Luke 19:41). In fact, Nehemiah was like the Lord Jesus in that he willingly shared the burden that was crushing others (Psalm 69:9; Rom 15:3).

When God puts a burden on your heart, don't try to escape it; for if you do, you may miss the blessing He has planned for you. Our tears water the seeds of providence that God has planted on our paths, and without our tears, those seeds could never grow and produce fruit.

A third way Nehemiah demonstrated that he cared is that he prayed (Neh. 1:5-10). This prayer is the first of twelve instances of prayer recorded in this book. It is obvious that Nehemiah was a man of faith who depended wholly on the Lord to help him accomplish the work He had called him to do.

His prayer is a model of how to be honest about one's grief, and demonstrates how to move beyond it in order to discover what calling God has for us through that grief. The prayers of Nehemiah that lasted "for some days" included the celebration and praise of God, even in the midst of the man's grief (vv. 5-6). Nehemiah confesses the sins of his people, his family's, and his own which had contributed to the present disaster (vv. 6-7)! I "confess the sins of the children of Israel which we have sinned against You. Both my father's house and I have sinned," he prayed.

In his praying, Nehemiah is not beneath reminding God of the commitments the Lord has made to Israel and especially the promise, "I will gather them from there, and bring them to the place which I have chosen as a dwelling for My name." Claiming that promise, Nehemiah asks God to show him – through his grief – what God wants him and God's other servants to do about the city (vv. 10-11).

Nehemiah does not yet have a clear-cut plan of action for dealing with Jerusalem's dilemma. He does know, however, the next risky step of faith God is asking him to take. In taking that step, Nehemiah demonstrates a fourth way of caring and that is to volunteer. So he prays God's favor upon that step: "let Your servant prosper this day, I pray, and grant him mercy in the sight of (the king)."

Now comes one of the most striking statements in the book of Nehemiah – striking for its simplicity and directness: "For I was the king's cupbearer" (v. 11). What was the cupbearer, and why does Nehemiah mention it at this point in the story?

This is not only a statement of fact. It is a statement of strategy. The cupbearer played quite an important role in the

Persian court. His status was ahead of courtiers, eunuchs, and gatekeepers of the palace, singers, and bakers – the people who made the court function. The role of the cupbearer was to select and present the wines and other drinks to the Persian king and queen during their meals, at state banquets, and on any other requested occasion. Because he was often in the Kings presence, strong attachments would develop. Because the cupbearer was also alone in the presence of the queen, he was a eunuch; it is reasonable to assume that Nehemiah was also a eunuch.

When Nehemiah states, therefore, "I was cupbearer to the king," he is also making more than an occupational observation. He is honestly appraising his situation and looking for possibilities in that situation.

Nehemiah's heart is broken over the fate of his city and as he has brought his pain to God in prayer, he feels increasingly that he is called by God to do something about that city. He does not have great amounts of money. He holds no political office. He is not a recognized leader of Persia or of Israel. But he is cupbearer to the king. Several times a day he is alone in the Persian emperor's presence. That king respects him, and his advice is appreciated.

This is who Nehemiah is. What, now, could he do with his position to address his concern for Jerusalem? Although highly irregular, he could take the risk of sharing his concern with the king. The risk was real, because if the king took offense, Nehemiah could lose not only his job but also his head (Esth. 4:9-11). But Jerusalem was worth the risk!

Chapter 1 of Nehemiah gives the essential grounds for undertaking God-empowered urban ministry. Nehemiah begins with himself. So should we. The starting point for us is with the question, "What makes me weep over my city?" If you answer that question with, "Nothing makes me weep over this city," you had better get out of urban ministry. You do not belong there. Only a man or woman who allows his or her heart to be broken with the pain and the plight of the hurting poor or powerful of the city belongs in urban ministry. To be effective in urban ministry, you must have a heart that is as big as the city itself. Such a heart develops only as you give yourself the permission to feel the pain of the city's people.

Then, like Nehemiah, bathe your tears in prayer. Prayer needs to flow from pain. When we cry to God over what breaks our hearts, He will make clear what He is calling us to do in the city. Only out of our brokenness and vulnerability can God show us how He wants to use us to empower people to "Rebuild the ancient ruins and restore the places long devastated; ... renew the ruined cities that have been devastated for generations" (Isa. 61:4).

Out of such willingness to open your life to the pain you feel about the city and out of your willingness to bathe your tears in prayer, God will lead you to honestly appraise your situation and look for new possibilities! You will discover, in God's timing, how God is calling you to contribute to the effort of empowering and liberating the city's broken. Also, you will be enabled to take the risky step of faith that takes you from reflection and quiet nurturing of pain to the action needed to deal with the issue.

It is terribly important, however, that you not rush the incubation of the pain. It is important that you take your time in perceiving and understanding God's call to do ministry in a new way in the city. Rushing the incubation will only bring a premature effort, a ministry not sufficiently grounded in God's struggle with you, which will provide the depth necessary for a sustaining work of empowerment and liberation.

It has well been said that prayer is not getting man's will done in heaven but getting God's will done on earth. However, for God's will to be done on earth, He needs people to be available for Him to use. God does "exceedingly above all that we ask or think, according to the power that works in us" (Eph. 3:20). If God is going to answer prayer, He must start by working in the one doing the praying! He works in us and through us to help us see our prayers answered.

While Nehemiah was praying, his burden for Jerusalem became greater and his vision of what needed to be done became clearer. Real prayer keeps your heart and your head in balance so that your burden doesn't make you impatient, thus running ahead of the Lord and ruining everything. As we pray, God tells us what to do, when to do it, and how to do it. All are important to the accomplishing of the will of God.

The day finally came where Nehemiah could keep it secret no longer. The call was brought forth as if it were a birth. He went to the king to express his pain.

Discussion Questions

1. What was the condition of the Jews living in Jerusalem? Consider their physical, emotional, spiritual and financial condition.
2. What was Nehemiah's reaction to the news?
3. What action plan did Nehemiah respond with?
4. Why do you think God called Nehemiah?
5. What principles do you see in Nehemiah's prayer that can be applied to your life?
6. In personal reflection, what does it take to go from indifference to concern?
7. How might God use the circumstances of your life to shape your calling?

CHAPTER 2
COMMITTING TO ACTION

Someone once said that there are 3 kinds of people in the world: Those who don't know what's happening; those who watch what's happening; and those who make things happen. Nehemiah's life is a classic example of the blend of God's blessing and man's diligence. He made things happen.

We must always keep in mind the balance between God's sovereignty and human responsibility. Some visionaries urge us to trust God for big things and not to be cautious. They challenge us "to step out of the boat in faith" and not limit what God can do. While pragmatists argue for the wisdom of fiscal prudence, to them, faith budgets that go beyond the present realities, present an ill-advised testing of God – not faithful stewardship. The visionary sees the possibility of what could be; the pragmatist is rooted in what truly exists. Both kinds of leaders are needed. The kind of disagreement that can develop because of their difference of viewing leadership responsibilities can be carried out in an attitude of love and mutual respect. Both visionaries and pragmatists represent a divergence in leadership values and practices. Some leaders major in spiritual disciplines of prayer and Bible study. Others exercise practical wisdom and down-to-earth basics. Some people are prejudice towards one style. Only few balance the two sides of leadership: the spiritual and the pragmatic, the divine/human responsibility.

Nehemiah first introduces himself as a spiritual leader whose vulnerable heart breaks over the dim state of God's people.

Through many tears, he shares his heart with God in extended periods of intense prayer. If we only read Nehemiah I, we might be tempted to classify Nehemiah among the visionaries whose minds are fixed on the things above, not on the practicalities of daily living.

But the second chapter of Nehemiah shows us a different side of Nehemiah. He plays out a careful strategy in preparing for rebuilding the wall of Jerusalem.

Nehemiah went to the King; he looked sufficiently downcast that the king asked, "Why does your face look so sad when you are not ill? This can be nothing but sadness of heart" (Neh. 2:2). So it was that Nehemiah shared with the king his burden, and the king responded to Nehemiah's pain. The response was to approve Nehemiah's request.

> Nehemiah 2:4-5 (NKJV)
> [4] Then the king said to me, "What do you request?" So I prayed to the God of heaven. [5] And I said to the king, "If it pleases the king, and if your servant has found favor in your sight, I ask that you send me to Judah, to the city of my fathers' tombs, that I may rebuild it."

With the king's permission granted, Nehemiah also gained the support of the queen (v. 6), the governors of Trans-Euphrates (v. 7), the keeper of the king's forest (v. 8), and strategic army and cavalry officers (v. 9). When he arrived in Jerusalem, Nehemiah moved in among the people, lived among them without telling them what he wanted to do (vv. 11-12), spent considerable time studying the situation, and seriously visited with the people (vv. 13-16).

What was Nehemiah doing? He was building the foundation upon which all the rest of his ministry in Jerusalem would be based. He was building his network. The success of everything else that he would do was built on the strength of the foundation he laid in those networks.

Networking is the first organizational task any urban pastor needs to do in his or her community. It is also perhaps the most important task. For on the strength of his or her networks will stand or fall the ministry. This is not to say that prayer and following God's instruction is not most important, only demonstrating the importance from a physical organizational level.

What is networking? It is the building and maintaining of those contacts, which will enable all of those in that network to carry out ministry more effectively to and with the exploited, the pagans, and the church in that city. Networking is the intentional systematic visiting of the people in a community by pastor and church people which lead to that community's organizing of itself to cope with its most substantive problems. That is what Nehemiah did – and what we are called to do also.

If networking is building upon biblical foundations – such as we observe here in Nehemiah's story, it will enable the urban church to reorder and prioritize its life and mission so that it will be able to join effectively with the poor and exploited of its city in their (and perhaps in the church's) liberation. By so joining in common cause, the church will gain the credibility to proclaim the Gospel to those who have formerly despised it.

Underlying the biblical concept of networking is the essential assumption that all human beings, however uneducated, exploited, and beaten down by life, have a greater capacity to understand and act upon their situation than the most highly informed or sympathetic outsider. Every human being, no matter how deprived, is created in the image of God and as such is no less innately capable of determining his future than the most highly educated and self-determined individual.

Nehemiah was not the only biblical net worker: among the finest were Moses and Paul. By God's Providence, both were prepared and used their preparation well.

Moses met God at the burning bush (Exod. 3:1-4:17). God had carefully prepared him for the task awaiting him. "Who am I, that I should go to Pharaoh and bring the Israelites out of Egypt?" Moses asked God incredulously (3:11). But God knew why He had chosen this apparently forgotten shepherd on the backside of the desert. As the son of a Hebrew slave, Moses had been miraculously delivered from Egyptian infanticide (Exod. 1:8-2:7) and had been subsequently well educated (Ex. 2:8-10). His commitment to the Jews and to their liberation was so great that he would later risk his own life and career in order to rescue an Israelite in distress (Exod. 2:11-15). It could truly be said of Moses that he was Hebrew of the Hebrews.

Moses was also an Egyptian of the Egyptians, however. "When the child grew older," Exodus 2:10 tells us, "(his Hebrew mother) took him to Pharaoh's daughter and he became her son. She named him Moses, saying, 'I drew him out of the water.'" Moses was, according to Josephus, considered a prince of Egypt, a member of the royal family. The treasures of Egypt and its political influence as the world's most powerful nation were all available to him (Heb. 11:24-26). Tradition has it that Moses was one of Egypt's most competent generals who successfully led a campaign against the Ethiopians. This was a man who understood the Egyptians – how they thought, what they prioritized, how they organized themselves. Even as a shepherd of the backside of the desert, Moses had access to the Pharaoh, whom he could later confront demanding, "Let my people go!" And once the Israelites had been let go, Moses had the Egyptian knowledge to organize this great host for a march across the desert.

Finally, Moses was a man of the desert. For forty years he had lived in the desert, made his livelihood by herding sheep, married and raised a family there. As well, he had entered into the family of Jethro, the priest of Midian who taught him how to survive in the desert and later helped him to organize and administer the vast company of freed slaves from Egypt (Exod. 18:13-27). From his desert associates, Moses was spiritually taught and strengthened so that he was prepared to lead his people through the forty years of wilderness wanderings.

Once Moses met God at the burning bush and received his vocation for the remainder of his life, it is intriguing to note how Moses used the network he had built over the years. Aaron, his brother and a Levite leader, provided him credibility and entrée to the Hebrew people. He used his contacts in Egypt to do what no other Israelite could do – enter Pharaoh's presence at will. Moses used Joshua and Caleb as lieutenants to organize the people; he used his father-in-law to train Israel's leaders in desert survival. Without the network Moses had built over the years, without his continuing ability to network during his confrontation with Pharaoh, and, without his ability to lead the people during their forty years in the desert, Israel's exodus from Egypt could never have happened. But in God's Providence, He prepared Moses for this very thing.

The Apostle Paul is a New Testament example of remarkable networking. Like Moses, Paul was a man magnificently prepared by God for the vocation to which God had called him. He was a man who thoroughly understood and was totally devoted to the Jewish faith and nation. In his own words, he testified, "(I was) circumcised on the eighth day, of the people of Israel, of the tribe of Benjamin, a Hebrew of the Hebrews; in regard to the law, a Pharisee; as for zeal, persecuting the church; as for legalistic righteousness, faultless" (Phil. 3:5-6).

At the same time, Paul was a man who understood and appreciated the Gentiles. Born and raised in the gentile city of Tarsus, Paul was a Roman citizen – a political lever he would use often for the sake of the church and his vocation. He understood the Greek culture, Roman law, gentile society, pagan religions, and even Roman sports. He therefore knew profoundly the people to whom he had been called to minister. No wonder Paul could write, "To the Jews I became like a Jew, to win the Jews ... To those not having the law I became like one not having the law ... so as to win those not having the law. To the weak I became weak, to win the weak. I have become all things to all men so that by all possible means I might save some" (1 Cor. 9:20-22).

When Paul was converted to Christ, with these words God sent Ananias to him: "Go (to Paul)! This man is my chosen instrument to carry my name before the Gentiles and their kings and before the people of Israel" (Acts 9:15). This was exactly what Paul did. For the remainder of his life, Paul became a tireless evangelist, spreading the Gospel throughout Judah, but primarily into the Gentile world. Paul's three successful missionary journeys into the pagan Roman Empire transformed Christianity from a Jewish sect into a worldwide faith for Jew and Gentile alike.

The effectiveness of these journeys was significantly enhanced by Paul's networking skills. The leaders he would gather from across the Roman Empire for evangelistic thrusts, his capacity to adapt his message to the people with whom he was dealing (evidencing his great appreciation and knowledge of their respective cultures), his building of an empire-wide network of skilled urban pastors and leaders who could be sent to troubled churches, his strategy for planting and growing churches in great urban centers, and his ability to deal with his protagonists testified to his skill. Paul was a supreme networker.

How can networking be done effectively in the city? Networking is based upon the living out of the Incarnation in the neighborhood in which your church has been placed by God to do. That means living among the people. An incarnational ministry is one which casts its lot with the neighborhood's people, working among them, spending time visiting with them, walking the streets, coming to know, caring about, and loving them. Networking is built upon this incarnational foundation.

Church leaders can visit people in their community: other pastors, business leaders, local politicians and party leaders, educators and service providers, but primarily they need to be with ordinary folks. What are you seeking to accomplish by networking? Essentially, you are seeking to learn about the community from its residents and those who work in it. From them you discover the issues about which they are concerned. You can identify who the community's real leaders are – the gatekeepers, caretakers, flak catchers, and brokers who make a community live (rarely are the real leaders of an urban community its formal leadership; those people only think they are the real leaders). We seek to uncover the people in the community who have a real burden for it and/or for one of its primary issues.

Why would a pastor and church want to learn such things from the community's people? If the church is going to minister effectively in its community, it must be addressing the issues the people perceive to be the issues; no other issues really exist. If the church is going to join with the people in dealing with these issues, it is necessary to have the real leaders of the community involved; otherwise any such effort lacks acceptance and credibility in the neighborhood's eyes. If the church and community are to deal with those issues, the people who have a real burden for those issues need to be involved in planning and undertaking the actions to address those issues. They are the people who care most about an issue and thus are the ones most motivated to do something about it.

How do you discover the people's issues, the community's leadership, the people who care? You ask the people! They will tell you. But you will not attain information from them until you have first invested yourself in them by living among them. Such information sharing comes as the end product of trust.

What does networking do for the urban church?

- It builds and nurtures a wide and steadily expanding system of relationships with the true leaders, concerned people and groups, and the ordinary folk of your community.
- It identifies those people in the community with whom your pastor or your church may want to build relationships.
- It influences the preaching and teaching of the church (as the church seeks to be responsive to the issues and needs uncovered in the community).
- It influences the church's plans and programs in and for the community.
- It affects the interior life of the church, sometimes in profound ways.
- It creates a community awareness of and respect for your church, and adds significantly to your church's credibility by creating a community consciousness of your church.
- It identifies possible future evangelistic contacts.

- It either confirms or requires the church to adjust the research it may have gathered on the community.

Most of all, however, what networking can do for your church is to prepare it to take that next risky step of faith that can transform its ministry and its relationship with your community and city. That is the next step that Nehemiah takes.

Shortly after Nehemiah arrived in Jerusalem, he set out on a secret mission to survey the broken wall. He took only "a few men" (v. 12), presumably those he could trust. His journey was only around a portion of the wall (the southern portion). Obviously, once he saw part of the wall, he had a good idea of the condition of the rest. This short passage reveals Nehemiah as a careful strategist with a shrewd sense of timing. He wanted to evaluate the scope of the work that awaited him. He did not want to draw attention to himself or give away his plans too early. He waited for just the right time to announce his plans to the people of Judah. He realized that by making a careful survey of the wall before gaining popular support, he would be ready to capitalize upon the people's initial enthusiasm. After appraising the condition of the wall, Nehemiah is ready to speak to the Jews of Jerusalem and the surrounding region and unveil God's plan for the city.

Discussion Questions

1. How much time elapsed between the time Nehemiah learned of the state of Jerusalem and his request of help from the king? What does this speak of walking in the time table of the Lord?
2. How did Nehemiah address the king and in what manner did he phrase his concern that the king might be sympathetic to his concern? What response and provision was given to Nehemiah?
3. How had Nehemiah's faithful service prepared him to be able to request such a great thing? How did Nehemiah translate the vision he had to the Jewish community?
4. In Your own community, what principles can you derive from this chapter that would be applicable to you?

CHAPTER 3
BUILDING WITH A TEAM

Having completed both his networking and his original research, Nehemiah gathered together "the priests ... nobles ... officials [and] any others who would be doing the work" (Neh. 2:16) – that is, the powerful and the people. Then a remarkable thing happened.

> Nehemiah 2:17-18 (NKJV)
> [17] Then I said to them, "You see the distress that we *are* in, how Jerusalem *lies* waste, and its gates are burned with fire. Come and let us build the wall of Jerusalem, that we may no longer be a reproach." [18] And I told them of the hand of my God which had been good upon me, and also of the king's words that he had spoken to me. So they said, "Let us rise up and build." Then they set their hands to *this* good *work*.

Based on his networking with the people and the officials, and based upon his own personal research, Nehemiah identifies the issue the people feel is most pressing: their sense of vulnerability due to their broken and ruined walls. As we will discover later on in this study, the broken-down walls of Jerusalem were not the real issue, but it was the issue the people felt the most; it was their most urgent issue. Therefore, it was the issue around which to organize the community.

Nehemiah organized the people around that issue. He said to them, "You see the trouble we are in: Jerusalem lies in ruins and its gates have been burned with fire." You can imagine the heads nodding in agreement as he spoke; somebody finally had the courage to say openly what all of them had all been feeling covertly.

Then Nehemiah, in essence, said to the people, "What are we going to do about it?" Notice that he does not say, "This is what the king of Persia is going to do about it," nor does he say, "This is what the priest or the local officials are going to do about it." He says, "Let us rebuild the wall of Jerusalem. Let us assume responsibility for our own situation, and do something about it."

Nehemiah also testified to "the gracious hand of my God upon me and what the king had said to me." In other words, Nehemiah assured them that they did not stand alone in the task of rebuilding the walls. The emperor of the entire Persian Empire was standing behind the project, and not just with his personal endorsement, but by his funding and provision of much of the materials for the project (Neh. 2:7-9). Moreover, God had blessed this endeavor so it was obvious that the Lord was behind the effort.

Neither king nor God would rebuild the walls, however. God and king would provide all the support necessary for the project to be completed. But it would be up to the Israelites living in Jerusalem to assume responsibility for their own situation and actually rebuild their walls.

Nehemiah was obeying the supreme law of community empowerment, a law consistently disobeyed or ignored by the church. The primary principles of undertaking truly effective and godly community ministry are these:

- The people who are best able to deal with a problem are the people most affected by that problem (see Acts 6).
- People who are excluded from full participation in the social, economic, or political life of their city or community can be empowered to participate only when they act collectively.

When most churches decide to minister to the people of their community, the members take it upon themselves to study that community and determine its primary issues and needs. Then, based on their findings, the church selects and determines the project or program needed to solve that problem or address that need. Once the church has decided what the solution needs to be, it goes ahead and implements, operates, and maintains that program.

Such an approach to community ministry is destined to fail! In this scheme, the ownership of the problem, the solution, and the program to implement that solution lies in the church – not the people. It is the church's program. The people of the community have no ownership in it. They may attend it and participate in it, but they will always be spectators and clients, never participants and goal-owners.

The church may want the community's people to become that program's goal-owners and may urge the people to provide leadership to the program. In fact, that may be an integral part of the programmatic plan, but the people will not assume that role in the program. The church will probably never be able to determine why the people of the community use but will not run the church's program because it will always perceive its intentions as having been honorable and God-inspired. Instead, the church will blame the people for being lazy and not assuming responsibility. But they are not lazy or irresponsible, just disenfranchised. Disenfranchised people always resist programmatic leadership by remaining spectators and clients.

The fate of the program is inevitable. It will function successfully as long as the church is willing to commit people, money, materials, and building to make it successful. But it will eventually "burn out." Once programmatic exhaustion has occurred and the well-intentioned pastor can no longer get sufficient volunteers or money or resources to maintain the program, that program will die.

It is the destructive tendency of the church to do ministry for a neighborhood's people, particularly the poor. But who then is in control? When we do ministry for the poor, the church is in control. The church decides what the people's problem is, what the solution should be, and what the project should be to implement that solution. The church is deciding everything. Therefore, even though that program might minister effectively to the physical or economic needs of the poor, it has actually pushed them down and enervated them further because it has deprived the poor of self-empowerment.

What, then, should the church do in the city? How should it address issues of health care, longevity and infant mortality, stress, environmental pollution, housing, economic development, advocacy, empowerment, stewardship of the city, relationship with God, and shalom with neighbor? Let it follow the example of Nehemiah. Let it follow the example of Paul. Do not do things for people! Do not come into Jerusalem with all the King's workers, money, materials, and supplies and rebuild the walls for them. Instead say to them, "Let us rebuild the walls together," and join in with the people as they collectively take charge of their own situation and rebuild the walls themselves. Only the people who are most affected by a problem can best deal with that problem. And they can best deal with that problem only when they work on it collectively.

True urban ministry will not occur when churches develop projects for the poor. True and effective urban ministry exists only when the city's churches work together with the poor to identify their needs and determine the actions the poor and the churches need to take together. Only out of such atmosphere will ministry by the poor occur for their own development. That is the approach that empowers people – that enables them to deal effectively with their own problems. That is the role of servant leadership to which the church is called in the city. And that is the process which enables the urban communities of the poor and of the church to minister to each other and, consequently, to set each other free!

Because the church does not often appreciate this way of looking at ministry, most city ministries make the same fateful error of taking a programmatic approach. Thank God Nehemiah did not make that mistake. Jerusalem may never have been rebuilt, Israel might not have been saved from disintegration, and Jesus would never have had a city to come and save!

How does Nehemiah empower the people of Jerusalem so that they can solve their own deteriorating situation? Already, he has:

- Allowed their plight to burn into his own soul to such a degree that he is obsessed with bringing about their empowerment.
- Networked with the powerful in order to gain their personal support, money, and resources.
- Networked with the people in order to ascertain what they perceived as their city's most urgent and immediate issues.
- Personally researched the situation to determine the accuracy of both his perception and the people's perception of their most urgent issue.
- Challenged and inspired the people to take charge of their own situation.

Now what? Where does Nehemiah go from here? How does he actually organize them to rebuild their own walls? Chapter 3 of the book of Nehemiah presents Nehemiah's action-plan.

Nehemiah 3:1-2 (NKJV)
^{1} Then Eliashib the high priest rose up with his brethren the priests and built the Sheep Gate; they consecrated it and hung its doors. They built as far as the Tower of the Hundred, *and* consecrated it, then as far as the Tower of Hananel. ^{2} Next to *Eliashib* the men of Jericho built. And next to them Zaccur the son of Imri built. ...

Nehemiah 3:30-32 (NKJV)
^{30} ...After him Hananiah the son of Shelemiah, and Hanun, the sixth son of Zalaph, repaired another section. After him Meshullam the son of Berechiah made repairs in front of his dwelling. ^{31} After him Malchijah, one of the goldsmiths, made repairs as far as the house of the Nethinim and of the merchants, in front of the Miphkad Gate, and as far as the

upper room at the corner. ³² And between the upper room at the corner, as far as the Sheep Gate, the goldsmiths and the merchants made repairs.

What initially appears to be a list of the people and families who worked on the wall is actually the people's action plan. If you trace on a map of Jerusalem each group's repair work, you will discover that the wall around the entire city has been repaired, beginning and ending with the Sheep Gate. After his initiating challenge to the citizens of Jerusalem, Nehemiah organized the people to accomplish the initial action. They were, together, rebuilding the entire perimeter wall of the city. Once the people began to rebuild their wall, they take charge of their own situation.

There is no indication from the text that the plan of action was Nehemiah's. All it tells us is that Nehemiah challenged them to rebuild those walls and defended the people against their critics. Most likely, it was the people who developed the plan of action – not by sitting around at endless meetings, but by getting to work!

With over forty-four groups in place, there was no breech of construction activity in the wall. People were assigned by residence (v. 21, 23, 24, 28-30). There are at least four reasons why this kind of coordinated plan might have been put in place:

- People who were assigned to sections of the wall near their homes would be personally involved and more highly motivated.
- People would not have to travel to another part of the city to do the job, wasting valuable time.
- In case of attack, these people would not be tempted to leave their posts but would stay and protect their families.
- The task would be a family effort, using all available talent.

By arranging for each worker to be close to home, it made it easy for them to get to work, be sustained on the job, and safeguard those who were nearest and dearest to them. This relieved each worker of any unnecessary anxiety. It also insured that each person would put his best effort into what he was doing.

Commuters were assigned to sections of the wall where there weren't many homes (v. 2, 5, 7). They were asked to complete tasks that could not be as conveniently handled by the permanent residents of Jerusalem. People were also assigned specific areas that related to their vocation. For example "Eliashib the High Priest" and "His brothers" were assigned to rebuild the "Sheep Gate" (v. 1). This would be an assignment that would be close to their hearts.

The people did not simply work on the walls. They spent time, as well, reflecting on their activity together – particularly when they met opposition from within or from outside (Neh. 4:6-14; 5:1-7). Early in the empowering process, Nehemiah built in the factor of community reflection and action. That process continued long after the completion of the walls and became the base by which Nehemiah led the people of Jerusalem into profound community reformation.

The example of Nehemiah reminds us that leaders of God's people are charged with the responsibility of mobilizing and empowering the people to do God's work. This does not mean, however that we should not get our hands dirty with tangible acts of service. Nehemiah 3 portrays leaders, even the high priest, who got involved in building the wall. People demonstrated their seriousness with their actions. Almost everyone was involved in this building project. Those who were experienced and qualified participated. Leaders, heads of households, officials supervised the rebuilding of certain sections of the wall. People from all ages and all walks of life participated: men, women and children (v. 12), priests (v. 1), goldsmiths (v. 8), perfumers (v. 8), temple servants (v. 26) and merchants (v. 32). Only a few exceptions were noted such as the Tekoite nobles.

Reflections on Nehemiah 3:1-22

One of the first things of importance to see is that God works through people. Rebuilding the walls of Jerusalem was God's work.

God stirred up Nehemiah in Chapter 1. He enabled him in Chapter 2. Nehemiah confessed God's hand (Neh. 2:20; 6:16). But God worked through people. Nehemiah chapter 3 is a reminder to us that the work of God happens when the people of God labor.

Too often we use the assurance that "God wants to do this work" as an excuse not to act ourselves. Yes, God wants to bring the lost to faith. Yes, He desires justice for the oppressed. But this does not free us from all responsibility. In fact, it places the responsibility squarely with us because as Christians we are called to do the work of God in this world. Knowing that God works through us should encourage us, especially when we labor faithfully without necessarily feeling God's assistance. It should also motivate us to get busy with God's business.

The second thing we learn is that Nehemiah demonstrated balanced and strategic leadership. Based on a spiritual foundation of prayer (Neh. 1:4-11) he organized effectively and delegated thoroughly. Over forty-four different groups worked on different sections of the wall. Nehemiah succeeded at one of the essential yet complex tasks of leadership: to translate broad vision into measurable, bite-sized projects.

Those who are called to lead often try to do it all themselves. Delegating responsibility requires time and effort. The example of Nehemiah reminds us that leaders of God's people are charged with the responsibility of mobilizing and empowering the people to do God's work (Eph. 4:12).

This does not mean, however, that I should not get my hands dirty with tangible acts of service. Nehemiah chapter 3 portrays leaders, even the high priest, who willingly became involved in building the wall. When we who lead consider ourselves above the fray, we act more like the Tekoite nobles than like the majority of the Judean leaders who were willing to get their hands dirty to accomplish God's work.

The third lesson we can glean is that the work of God happens most effectively when everyone participates. Judeans of both genders, from various occupations, diverse locations, and social classes – all joined in the great restoration project. The wall was completed in record time (Neh. 6:15) because everybody worked hard.

If it is the responsibility of people to do God's work, then it is the responsibility of leaders to help them accomplish that work. Many people are willing, but they simply don't know where to serve – they can't find their place in the wall. Christians serve according to the direction and empowerment of the Sovereign Spirit. Recognizing the sovereignty of God's Spirit and the responsibility we share, we need to do the following: pray for God's guidance (look around, God often calls us into ministry right where we are), consult with Christian friends, receive guidance from church leaders, and follow your passion.

Lastly, we must find our meaning in our piece of the wall. God intends to work in the world through us. The church of Christ needs the participation of each member, just as each member needs to experience the joy and fulfillment of contributing to God's work. We spend so much of our lives on projects destroyed "by moth and rust" (Matt. 6:19). What a fulfilling contrast to see our efforts contribute to God's great work on earth!

We all need to experience the joyful sense of contributing to God's work. Our lives find ultimate meaning in knowing that we have labored – as parents, as church workers, as doers of justice, as communicators of God's truth and love – for what will last. Consider building your part of the wall so that together we can fulfill God's purposes.

Building Coalitions in Our Communities

As a result of networking in your local community, you can take note of the issues most often raised by people. Then go to the real leaders and the concerned people who have most often voiced those concerns. Ask them to come together to discuss the issues, and share with them the names of pivotal people from the community that are also committed to those issues.

Get together and reflect about the specific issue. Seek to understand the issue and examine the community need. Soon in the process introduce the question, "What are we going to do about it?" From that question, the group can determine the first action or project that they are willing to undertake.

It is important in this early stage of empowerment that the fledging coalition gets accustomed to winning. An integral problem for the poor and the marginalized of the city is that they have lost at the hands of the system all their lives. Therefore, victory is imperative in order to communicate to that neighborhood, the community groups, and churches that together they can win! Consequently, as the coalition selects its initial actions, it needs to choose activities that cannot fail. And these projects should be ones for which the coalition assumes full responsibility.

During that initial action, and particularly after it, the coalition gathers to reflect upon it. What did they learn from it? What went well? Why? What went poorly? Why? What should we pat ourselves on the back about? What can we learn about ourselves, our community, our community groups, etc.? Such reflection should then lead to the determination of the next, and slightly more challenging, action. That action should lead to deeper reflection. This should lead to an even deeper action, continued with more profound reflection, and so on and on and on. Three things will inevitably come out of this kind of community empowerment:

- The coalition will move through an ever-deepening process of reflection and action.
- Natural leadership will rise like cream to the top of the coalitions. This leadership can be called forth, encouraged, and strengthened through various leadership-training activities, and used to support the community empowerment process. Incidentally, this was the one substantive mistake Nehemiah made in his organizing of the Jerusalem community; he did not identify, call forth, encourage, and use other leaders. The result was a near-disastrous power vacuum, which, upon Nehemiah's return to the court of the

Persian king, almost destroyed that noble experiment (Neh. 13:4-31).
- Such action and reflection will quickly reveal to coalitions organized around different community issues that they will more effectively reach their respective objectives by working together and enabling each other.

Using this process, the church acts as partner-servant with the people and groups of its community. Through its networking, it identifies the real issues of the people of that community and the pivotal leaders and motivated community people who can address these issues. The church acts to pull these people together into coalitions formed around the issues the people have identified as most important. Then the church joins with the coalition to analyze the issues and reflect on the more substantive forces lying behind those issues. It joins with the coalition to share in the development and implementation of projects and actions the coalition and community see as necessary. The community will own such projects and the people will invest significant effort to make those projects work. The church can be part of that entire process, participating with the community in the implementation of those projects and providing those resources the church is best equipped to provide and for which the community asks. Thus, the church will be an integral part of the reformation of that community, will be respected and trusted in that enabling role, and will have the permission of the community to share that faith which makes such selfless ministry possible.

Discussion Questions

1. How important is team ministry?
2. What are some of the ways that Nehemiah used to motivate the people of Jerusalem?
3. How did Nehemiah get the people of Jerusalem to take ownership of the building process?

4. How does this chapter relate to other New Testament Scriptures such as Eph. 4; Rom. 12, and 1 Cor. 12?
5. How might Psalm 133 relate to this chapter?

CHAPTER 4
LEADING DESPITE OPPOSITION

Empowerment of the poor and marginalized will inevitably create conflict. Those who hold power will not like the poor or marginalized taking charge of their situation (and thus taking power from the power-brokers). Those who have always been beaten down by life will often be tempted to abuse their newly discovered power, for the poor and the marginalized are as capable of doing evil as are people of power! This was one of the struggles of the children of Israel in the wilderness, as they only had the model of Pharaoh in their mind as they dealt with one another and faced the enemy of God (see Exodus 18).

Conflict can be a sign that effective empowerment of the ordinary people of a community or city is occurring. If those who hold the power and benefit from the maintenance of the status quo begin to resist the work of the community's organization, and if those in the organization seek to misuse their power, then empowerment is working! This was as true for Nehemiah as it is for the church working among the disadvantaged today.

Nehemiah knew at "just when you thought it was safe" syndrome all too well. In reviewing Nehemiah chapters 2 and 3, we see everything running smoothly. The king had blessed Nehemiah's venture and provided permission, power, provision and protection. The people had rallied around Nehemiah and had begun to work energetically. We can see coordination, cooperation and commendation in progress. Suddenly in chapters 4-6, Nehemiah is confronted with opposition, not only from his enemies but also from his own people.

Opposition is not only evidence that God is blessing, but it is also an opportunity for us to grow. Satan wanted to use these problems as weapons to destroy the work, but God used them as tools to build His people. Charles Spurgeon said, "God had one Son without sin, but He never had a son without trial."

Chapters 4-6 describe at least nine different tactics that the enemy used to try to stop the work on the walls.

1. They attacked the Jewish people with ridicule (4:1-6)
2. Plots of war (v. 7-9)
3. This resulted in difficulties within the Jewish ranks: discouragement (v. 10),
4. Fear (v. 11-23), and
5. Selfishness (5:1-19).
6. When attacks on the people failed to stop the work the enemy tried compromise (6:1-4),
7. Slander (v. 5-9),
8. Treats (v. 10-14) and
9. Intrigue (v. 17-19)

None of these devices worked either. Here we can learn from Nehemiah's example how to overcome adversity in our lives and in our ministries.

Confronting Mockery – Nehemiah 4:1-6

Nehemiah 4:1-6 (NKJV)
[1] But it so happened, when Sanballat heard that we were rebuilding the wall, that he was furious and very indignant, and mocked the Jews. [2] And he spoke before his brethren and the army of Samaria, and said, "What are these feeble Jews doing? Will they fortify themselves? Will they offer sacrifices? Will they complete it in a day? Will they revive the stones from the heaps of rubbish—*stones* that are

burned?" ³ Now Tobiah the Ammonite *was* beside him, and he said, "Whatever they build, if even a fox goes up *on it,* he will break down their stone wall." ⁴ Hear, O our God, for we are despised; turn their reproach on their own heads, and give them as plunder to a land of captivity! ⁵ Do not cover their iniquity, and do not let their sin be blotted out from before You; for they have provoked *You* to anger before the builders. ⁶ So we built the wall, and the entire wall was joined together up to half its *height,* for the people had a mind to work.

Nehemiah's opponents, Sanballat and Tobiah, the Ammonite, appear once again. Like a general patrolling his troops, Sanballat mocked the Jews in a voice that must have been full of animosity and spite (v. 2). Tobiah, the Ammonite, added his denigration "whatever they build, if even a fox goes up on it, he will break down their stone wall" (v. 3).

Who were Sanballat, Tobiah, and the Arabs of whom Nehemiah speaks? Sanballat was the governor of Samaria, Tobiah was the governor of the Persian province of Trans-Jordan, and one of the Arabs referred to as Geshem was the highly influential father of an Arabian king (Kain of Kedar) who had united the Arabian tribes into a desert confederation (Neh. 2:10, 19). These men were the people responsible for maintaining order throughout Canaan and were nominally accountable to the Persian emperor. In addition, "the Arabs, the Ammonites and the men of Ashdod" were the peoples maintaining and benefiting from the trade and industry of the region by exploiting the Jews' cheap labor.

In other words, those resisting the action of the people of Jerusalem as they sought to improve their conditions were the political and economic establishments of Palestine – the primary system shaping the life of all the people around Jerusalem. The Sanballat's and Tobiah's of today take the form of bureaucrats who see any version of Christianity that challenges the status quo as subversive, unnecessary, unwise, and destructive rather than constructive in its thrust.

They value routine above revival – snuffing out spiritual life. Sanballat and Tobiah were "deeply disturbed that a man had come to seek the well-being of the children of Israel (Neh. 2:10). Perhaps Sanballat and Tobiah were not so disturbed by help for Israel as by the threat Nehemiah posed to their own self-aggrandizement. Many people are not concerned about others, only, about how things will affect them. Probably the fact that Nehemiah had an escort caused them to be more cautious, at least for the time being.

This was a thrust at morale. One of the oldest weapons of the enemy is an open attack with a barrage of words. What are these feeble Jews doing? Will they offer sacrifices? Will they pray up the wall? Ridicule needs no factual ammunition. On this occasion, the morale, which was attacked, was too well founded to be undermined. The words stung, but they produced not a quiver of indecision only indignation. Nehemiah responded with fervent prayer (v. 4-5).

Two aspects of Nehemiah's prayer deserve our attention. First, notice that Nehemiah prioritized prayer. When mocked, he did not shout back; he turned to God. In times of conflict and criticism is prayer on the top of your list of responses? Second, Nehemiah prayed honestly, not exactly a friendly neighborly prayer. He told God exactly what he wanted, with startling candor. God already knows what is on our hearts. By screening everything we say in prayer, we miss the vitality and transforming power of honest conversation with God.

Only when we can tell the truth to God in our prayers, no matter how unattractive the truth might be, we will enter into genuine, intimate relationship with God. God is big enough to hear prayers that authentically reveal our thoughts and emotions. Nehemiah's prayerful response achieved its purpose. Workers continued until one-half of the wall was reached (v. 6). In spite of insults from opposing leaders, "the people had a mind to work."

Opposition Through Discouragement
Nehemiah 4:7-23

When mockery failed to stop the rebuilding, the enemies of Judah threatened to attack (v. 8, 11). They did not intend to actually take control of the city but merely to "create confusion" (v. 8) and to "cause the work to cease" (v. 11). Sanballat and Tobiah had rallied a considerable alliance (including the Arabs, the Ammonites, and the Ashdodites). Nehemiah and his band were surrounded. Sanballat and the Samaritans were to the north. Tobiah and the Ammonites were to the east. The Arabs with Geshem (2:9) were to the south. The Ashdodites were to the west.

The failure of this impressive group to strike a single blow suggests "the king's letters" (Neh. 2:9) gave them pause. But their plotting, however, half-hearted, clearly included potential raids and harassments and had to be taken seriously.

Apparently, the threat of attack from the surrounding nations weakened the spirits of the Jews. "Then Judah said" refers to circulating, common gossip. The word on the street was: everybody is getting tired. All of the rubbish is getting in our way. While mockery had no effect, military intimidation did. The enemies kept issuing threats, promising to attack secretly in order to bring the rebuilding efforts to a halt (v. 11). As a result, frightened Jews from outlying areas, who felt particularly vulnerable, repeatedly complained of their fears to Nehemiah. "Ten times" probably means "again and again." The atmosphere of growing misgivings and unnerving rumors within the company could do as much damage as the enemy outside. Judah doubted their power to complete the task. They were thinking "we will not be able to do this ourselves." It was a natural sinking heart, at this halfway stage, and we are reminded that dead tiredness was not the least of these burdens.

Once again, Nehemiah responded by praying (v. 9). In addition, the Jews "set a watch against them day and night" and prepared for an attack. Taunts had been met by prayer and concentrated work, plots by prayer and guard duty (v. 7-9).

Stronger threats were dealt with by a general call to arms and the charge to "keep your minds on the Lord ... and fight" (v. 10-14). Now the temporary lull is accepted for what it is: a chance to start building again but not to disarm.

Nehemiah gathered the people together fully armed and ready for battle. By positioning this congregation "behind the lower parts of the wall, at the openings" (v. 13), Nehemiah guaranteed that their enemies would see the strength and readiness of the Jews. Once in place, Nehemiah delivered a rousing pep talk, calling on the people to keep their focus on God, who is "great and awesome" (v. 14). With their mind-set properly focused, the people of Judah were ready to fight for their families. They declared, "our God will fight for us" (v. 20). Recalling the words of Psalm 127, "Unless the Lord builds the house, they labor in vain who build it ... unless the Lord watches over the city ... the watchman stays up awake in vain."

This defensive strategy proved successful (v. 15). The principle in place was that every minute of daylight was now precious, and darkness must not undo the day's achievements. From that time forward, Nehemiah and his crew remained prepared for a surprise attack at all times. Half of Nehemiah's servants stood guard while others worked (Neh. 4:16). The builders bore arms while laboring on the wall (Neh. 4:13-18). A long distance communication system was deployed (Neh. 4:18-20). The workers camped in Jerusalem in order to protect the city (Neh. 4:21-22).

Reflections on Nehemiah 4:1-23

In Chapter 4, Nehemiah responds to his opponents with a combination of prayer and preparation for battle, balancing spiritual and pragmatic leadership. There is a tension between trusting God and taking steps to ensure security.

The New Testament teaches clearly that God's people should expect opposition because we are at war (Eph. 6:10-13). Christians are in a battle against spiritual forces. How do we prepare to oppose these spiritual forces? Paul gives us instruction in Ephesians 6:13-14.

Ephesians 6:13-14 (NKJV)
[13] Therefore take up the whole armor of God, that you may be able to withstand in the evil day, and having done all, to stand. [14] Stand therefore, having girded your waist with truth, having put on the breastplate of righteousness...

We prepare by putting on the whole armor of God: truth, righteousness, peace, faith, salvation and the Word of God. We should major on majors. Focus on the essentials of the Christian faith. Don't get hung up in the fine print. We prepare for spiritual warfare not by focusing on the devil and his forces, but by stressing the core aspects of Christian faith. Once we have prepared ourselves with the armor, how do we fight these spiritual battles? Let's look at Ephesians 6:18-20.

Ephesians 6:18-20 (NKJV)
[18] praying always with all prayer and supplication in the Spirit, being watchful to this end with all perseverance and supplication for all the saints— [19] and for me, that utterance may be given to me, that I may open my mouth boldly to make known the mystery of the gospel, [20] for which I am an ambassador in chains; that in it I may speak boldly, as I ought to speak.

Paul's instruction is clear: we fight by praying. Spiritual warfare entails other activities like planning, preaching and works of service. However, to disregard prayer is to discard our primary weapon. To fight effectively, we must recognize that prayer is more effective than multiple other activities.

Are we praying for our cities, leaders, schools and Christian leaders? Do we pray for our children? Do we pray individually and corporately? In the privacy of our prayer closets, do we pray honestly? Do we tell God the truth?

Nehemiah faced opposition, and so will we. Just when we think it is safe, a spiritual battle will come our way. Can we remember "the Lord great and awesome" (v. 14)? Can we rejoice in the fact that "our God will fight for us" (v. 20)? So, with expectation of victory, let us put on the armor and fight!

Discussion Questions

1. What areas of persecution are encountered in this chapter and what does Nehemiah do to overcome?
2. Who might these principles help you?
3. When we do God's work should we expect opposition?
4. What positive benefit does persecution produce in the life of the believer?
5. Translating vision into action takes work and perseverance. What have you learned in this chapter that can be applied to your life and ministry?

CHAPTER 5
A THREAT FROM WITHIN

When the enemy fails with his attacks from the outside, he then begins to attack from within, and one of his favorite weapons is selfishness. If he can get us thinking only about ourselves and what we want, then he will win the victory before we realize that he is even at work. Selfishness means putting myself at the center of everything and insisting on getting what I want when I want it. It means exploiting others so I can be happy and taking advantage of them just so I can have my own way. It is not only wanting my own way but expecting everybody else to want my way too.

Scripture speaks of both God and Satan "tempting" – that is, trying people out to see what is in them, testing them as students are tested in school examinations. We read that Jesus was tested by the devil (Matt. 4:1), and that God tempted Abraham (Gen. 22:1). The truth is that in every testing situation, both Satan and God are involved.

God tests us to bring forth excellence in discipleship, as Moses explained to the Israelites at the close of the wilderness wanderings:

> "Remember how your Lord and God led you all the way in the desert these forty years, to humble you and to test you in order to know what was in your heart, whether or not you would keep His commandments ... He gave you manna ... to humble and to test you" – to drill you, that is, in grateful,

confident, disciplined, submissive reliance on himself – "so that in the end it might go well with you" (Deut. 8:2, 16).

Satan, by contrast, tests us with a view to our ruin and destruction, as appears from Paul's reason for sending Timothy to strengthen and encourage the harassed Thessalonian Christians: "I was afraid that in some way the tempter might have tempted you and our efforts might have been useless" – in other words, Satan might have persuaded them to give up their faith and so ruin their souls (1 Thess. 3:2-5). Satan was, of course, with the Israelites in the desert, laboring to ensnare them in unbelief and lawlessness of various kinds and often succeeding in his purpose, in the short term at least; God was with the Thessalonians in the furnace, disciplining them for their good, that they might share His holiness (Heb. 12:10). Temptation is always two sided in this way, so whenever we are conscious of Satan seeking to pull us down, we should remind ourselves that God is present, too, to keep us steady and to build us up through the harrowing experience.

In Nehemiah 4 we saw Satan using three devices – psychological warfare, physical threats, and personal discouragement – to nullify Nehemiah's rebuilding project. In Nehemiah 5 and 6, we shall see him, having failed so far, turning his attention to Nehemiah in a more direct way, working to destroy him personally by discrediting him in his role as leader of God's people. If successful, God's work would be forfeited. Satan's opening ploy was subtle. It began with a generation of grievances that threatened to stop the work; there was also an attempt to smear Nehemiah and alienate him from the community as a whole.

A Great Outcry – Nehemiah 5:1-7

Nehemiah 5:1-7 (NKJV)
[1] And there was a great outcry of the people and their wives against their Jewish brethren. [2] For there were those who said, "We, our sons, and our daughters *are* many; therefore let us get grain, that we may eat and live." [3] There were also

some who said, "We have mortgaged our lands and vineyards and houses, that we might buy grain because of the famine." ⁴ There were also those who said, "We have borrowed money for the king's tax *on* our lands and vineyards. ⁵ Yet now our flesh *is* as the flesh of our brethren, our children as their children; and indeed we are forcing our sons and our daughters to be slaves, and *some* of our daughters have been brought into slavery. *It is* not in our power *to redeem them,* for other men have our lands and vineyards." ⁶ And I became very angry when I heard their outcry and these words. ⁷ After serious thought, I rebuked the nobles and rulers, and said to them, "Each of you is exacting usury from his brother." So I called a great assembly against them.

In the midst of a "great work" (Neh. 4:19) for a "great God" (Neh. 1:5), a "great cry" (Neh. 5:1) was heard among the Jews. Just when Judah was finally able to withstand threats from outside, internal squabbles erupted. Just when it seemed safe to build again, the citizens of Judah cried out to Nehemiah with ominous complaints.

Just like all Palestine Jews, the Jewish nobles and officials had been living under the oppressive policies of Sanballat, Tobiah, Geshem, and "the Arabs, the Ammonites and the men of Ashdod." But given the chance, these middle-level Jewish leaders were taking advantage of their people's newly won self-determination to oppress their fellow Jews. Having gained some measure of independence, the oppressed had turned into the oppressors! They were practicing business in such a way that they were putting poorer Jews into economic subjection to them.

The text distinguishes these three groups of protesters. The first group complained: "We need food for our large families" (v. 2). These people owned no land and because of the famine that had been in the land were hungry. The second group complained: "We have mortgaged our property for food" (v. 3). Apparently inflation was on the rise, and prices were going higher. The combination of debt and inflation is enough to quickly wipe out a person's equity. Group three added: "We have borrowed money to pay our taxes" (v. 4). In order to borrow money, they had to give security, and this meant eventually losing their property.

Verse 5 may summarize a terrible complaint experienced by all three parties: due to financial hardships, they had been forced to sell their children into slavery. While slavery was not prohibited in the Law, it was strictly regulated (Exod. 21:2-11). For example, the Jews were commanded to regard their fellow Jews as hired laborers, not as slaves (Lev. 25:39-43). In Nehemiah's situation, the phrase "some of our daughters have been brought into slavery" (v. 5) implies in the original language either that their daughters had been forced to marry their owners or that they had been sexually molested.

Verse 3 mentions a famine on the land, which may or may not have been related to Nehemiah's building project. Judah's post-exilic history had not begun with Nehemiah's arrival, nor even with the great trouble and shame which were reported to him in Susa. His diverting of manpower from raising crops to raising walls may have been the final burden; it did not have to be the first. Nehemiah's project so distressed Judah's neighbors that trade between Jews and other regions probably stopped altogether. Then when these economic hardships overwhelmed the land, those with financial resources jumped at the chance to profit from the misfortune of their fellow Jews.

While the majority of citizens faced economic hardships, a few wealthy nobles and rulers (v. 7) took advantage of the situation. They loaned money to their fellow Jews and took property as security. From some, they even purchased their children as slaves.

What was Nehemiah to do? How was he to deal with the opposition of Palestine's political and economic systems to the rebuilding of the wall? How would he deal with the economic betrayal of God's people by God's people?

Responding to the Outcry – Nehemiah 5:6-13

When Nehemiah heard the people's cries, he "became very angry" (v. 6). He was angry over the injustice done to God's people. He took time to devote serious thought to what his response should be (v. 7). It is one thing to confront foreign enemies and quite something else to deal with your own people when they fight one another. Young Moses learned that it was easier to dispose of an Egyptian master then to reconcile two Jewish brothers (Exod. 2:11-15). Nehemiah showed true leadership in his response to the problem. He was not a politician who asked, "What is popular?", or a diplomat who asked, "What is safe?", but a true leader who asked, "What is right?"

Why didn't Nehemiah know about this scandalous economic problem sooner? Probably because he was so immersed in the one thing he came to do – the rebuilding of the walls – that he had no time to get involved in the internal affairs of the community. It is important to note that the building of the walls did not create these problems; it revealed them. Often when a church enters into a building program, problems surface that people didn't even know were there. A building program is demanding, it tests our faith, our patience, and our priorities, and while it brings out the best in some people, it can often bring out the worst in others.

Nehemiah responded by confronting "the nobles and rulers." "Each of you is exacting usury from his brother" (v. 7). Each of you is acting like a "pawnbroker" with his own brother. Israel went into bondage as an agricultural society and emerged in commerce.

After confronting the offenders directly, Nehemiah summoned "a great assembly" – including the accused, the victims, and others to serve as witnesses (v. 7). He confronted the nobles and rulers with the folly of their actions by listing the charges against them. Nehemiah appealed to:

1. Their love, by reminding them that they were robbing their own fellow Jews, not Gentiles (v. 7).

2. His appeal was based solidly on the Word of God, for the Law of Moses forbade Jews to exact interest from one another.
3. Nehemiah reminded them of God's redemptive purpose for Israel (Neh. 5:8). Were they now going to put their brethren into bondage?
4. Israel's witness to their Gentile neighbors was in question (v. 9), God called Israel to be a "light unto the Gentiles" (Isa. 42:6; 49:6), but their conduct was certainly anything but a witness to their pagan neighbors.
5. Nehemiah appealed to his own personal practice.

In light of the offense, Nehemiah called the lenders to "restore" all personal property held as security for loans (v. 11) and also to give back the "hundred" that had been charged (12% interest). In other words, lenders were to give back all profit made on the loans. The lenders agreed with a symbolic gesture – the fold of a garment was the ancient equivalent of a pocket. By emptying his fold while uttering these words, Nehemiah was stating: "If you don't do as you have promised, may God take away all of your possessions." The combination of these strategies was successful, and the passage ends on the positive note "then the people did according to this promise" (v. 13).

Nehemiah's Example of Sacrifice – Nehemiah 5:14-19

This passage provides several tidbits of historically significant material. Nehemiah was "governor of Judah" – 12 years. In looking at his example of leadership, we can summarize a few qualities in this section: he did not profit financially. He did not speculate or buy land. He did not collect "the governor's provisions" which was his right. Nehemiah's sensitivity to the "heavy bondage" already placed upon the people lead him to drain his personal resources rather then to add to the people's bondage (v. 18). He continued to be hospitable and feed all who ate at his table.

In typical style, Nehemiah ends this section with a prayer, asking God to "remember" him for all that he has done for Judah (v. 19). It does not matter what people think – it matters what God sees.

Reflections on Nehemiah 5:1-19

Without doubt, Christian leaders will face opposition and conflict, not only from outside agitators, but from internal agitators as well. How are we who lead to respond to criticism and conflict? If you are in a position of spiritual leadership, or ascribe to be, this chapter has some important lessons to review:

- To begin with, expect problems to arise among those you work with. Whenever you have people, you will have the potential for problems. Whenever God's work is prospering, the enemy sees to it that trouble begins. Don't be surprised when your people can't always get along with each other.
- Second, confront the problems courageously. "There is no problem so great that you can't ignore it"; this might be a good philosophy for a character in a comic strip, but it won't work in the Lord's service. Every problem that you ignore will only go underground, grow deeper roots, and bear bitter fruits. Pray for God's help and tackle the problem as soon as possible.
- Third, be sure that your own integrity is intact. A guilty conscience will rob you of the spiritual authority you need to give proper leadership, but every sacrifice you have made will give you the extra strength you need to defeat the enemy.
- Finally, see in every problem an opportunity for the Lord to work. Solving problems in ministry is not an intellectual exercise but a spiritual experience. If we depend only on the wisdom of this world, we may negate what God wants to do. All that we say and do must be motivated by love, controlled by truth, and done to the glory of God.

The calling of the assembly and the solving of the economic problems had interrupted the work on the wall, and now it was time for everybody to get back to his or her place on the wall. But Nehemiah's enemies would also be busy. This time they would aim their ammunition especially at Nehemiah and try to defeat him with four devilish devices.

Before we continue to look at the continued attacks on Nehemiah, we must first put something in perspective. Satan, through his agents devilish and human, assaults all Christians, and leaders supremely; they must learn to pray with Nehemiah, "Now strengthen my hands" (Neh. 6:9) – not only for the constructive ministry, corresponding to the building of Jerusalem's wall, but also for mortal combat, corresponding to the sequence of defensive measures against Jerusalem's enemies. When this is truly the prayer of our hearts, then the outcome of the conflict is assured, for leaders, no less than for others, caught in the fight. Those who seek God's strength will find it. The outcome will be salvation, not destruction: Satan will be thwarted and the church built up, and the God through whom all the work is done will be glorified.

Discussion Questions

1. What opposition is encountered in this chapter?
2. There is a difference between temptation and testing. What source does each come from and what are the intended results does each try to produce?
3. What strategies do you use to overcome temptation, or endure testing?
4. How is the authority of leadership dependant on your depth of character?
5. Problems encountered must be faced courageously. Explain how Jesus gave instruction in dealing with this in Matthew 18?
6. What have you learned in this chapter that will help you lead others?

CHAPTER 6
CONFRONTING PERSONAL ATTACKS

The enemy's main purpose was to generate fear in the heart of Nehemiah and his workers (Neh. 6:9, 13-14, 19), knowing that fear destroys faith and paralyzes life. Both Jesus (Luke 13:31-37) and Paul (Acts 21:10-14) had to face the specter of fear, and both overcame it by faith. Up to this point in time the building project has continued to move ahead in spite of frustrating opposition. There were challenges from the outside as neighboring opponents threatened Judah. There were challenges from within as internal strife threatened to destroy Judean unity. Now the threats are no longer against the nation. Instead they are directed at Nehemiah. Chapter six of Nehemiah, provides opportunity to learn how we should respond when we are attacked personally or are tempted to divert our attention from God's call upon our lives.

An Attempt to Discredit and Endanger Nehemiah
Nehemiah 6:1-4

The workers had almost finished the wall. All that remained was to hang the doors. Then Sanballat, Tobiah and Geshem the Arab (v. 1), who had opposed Nehemiah from the beginning (Neh. 2:10, 19), tried once again in desperation to derail the project. All of a sudden they want to help! What's wrong with this picture? Here is the bait – compromise. The enemy strategy is "if you can't whip them – join them and then take over." If the enemy can get a foothold, then he can start to weaken from within. His goal is for the work to fail.

Why did Nehemiah suspect ill will? Was it past experience? I think that it was the location of the meeting. When we don't trust someone we usually question his or her motives. Sanballat and Tobiah did not offer to come to Jerusalem – they invited Nehemiah to a distant region. The plain of Ono was located more than 25 miles northwest of Jerusalem. Ono would not be safe for Nehemiah. The trip alone would be at least a 2-day journey causing a distraction from finishing the wall. Ono was also a place of social unrest – a hostile region. Nehemiah could be jumped or killed. Wisely Nehemiah declined the meeting. He said, "I cannot leave with all my responsibilities." Four times he was invited – four times he declined.

How should we respond when we are faced with potentially distracting opportunities? By saying no. Nehemiah stated his priorities and commitments. He remained focused on the task at hand. How difficult is it to stay focused on what really matters? When we lose focus, we diminish our effectiveness. We can learn from Nehemiah to evaluate new opportunities in light of God's higher call upon our lives. We need to remember that staying focused means sometimes saying no.

Attempt to Libel Nehemiah – Nehemiah 6:5-9

Since Nehemiah refused to be distracted, Sanballat tried another approach to disrupt the work. Sanballat dispatched his servant with "an open letter" (v. 5). The Hebrew emphasizes that the correspondence was unsealed. Sanballat was less interested in communicating with Nehemiah than in spreading rumors through a libelous, unsealed letter. Sanballat's letter contained two libelous accusations: the Jews plan to rebel "against the Persians", and Nehemiah intends to become king (v. 6). Sanballat's primary purpose was not to inform on Nehemiah; rather, it was to incite division and disunity within Judah. No doubt he reasoned that if common Judeans began to see Nehemiah as a self-centered opportunist, they would stop supporting him and his building project. The accusations served Sanballat's purpose of denigrating Nehemiah. This power hungry man could not have comprehended Nehemiah's desire to serve Judah and to build the wall simply for Judah's good and for God's glory.

In every organization, there are gossipmongers, hovering like vultures, just waiting for tidbits or slander that they can chew, swallow, and then regurgitate. An anonymous wit has defined "gossip" as "news you have to hurry and tell someone else before you find out it isn't true!" Not only did his enemies falsely accuse Nehemiah of forming a rebellion, but they also said he was planning to make himself king and had prophets prepared to announce his coronation (v. 7). True to his character, Nehemiah simply dismissed their charges and prayed for strength (v. 9). There is no evidence that Nehemiah composed a letter of defense for the Persian King. Surely, he knew that this rumor could create havoc with the Persian King. Perhaps his character before the king and God's hand upon him is what he needed to rely on. He simply stated the truth as he knew it, prayed, and moved on.

Nehemiah trusted God for strength and protection, but he also trusted in the truth. Nehemiah seemed to believe that the truth would prevail without the investment of costly time and energy in defending his honor.

An Attempt to Disgrace Nehemiah
Nehemiah 6:10-14

The next attempt to distract Nehemiah originated from an obscure Jewish prophet named Shemaiah (v. 10). He was a secret informer to discredit Nehemiah. Tobiah and Sanballat, hired him (v. 12-13). Shemaiah prophesied to Nehemiah: your enemies "are coming to kill you." The prophet had a plan: let us meet together in the house of God, within the temple. He proposed that the leader of Judah hide, within the larger temple structure (the House of God), but specifically within the "temple" itself – in the Holy place just outside of the Holy of Holies. But Nehemiah is not a priest, and as such, had no right to enter the Holy Place. For someone to go into the Holy Place was punishable by death (Num. 18:7). If carried out, Shemaiah's proposal would disgrace Nehemiah in two ways. First, it would cause him to commit a ritual transgression by going where priests alone were allowed (Deut. 13:1-5; 18:20-22). Second, by hiding to save his own life, Nehemiah would be seen as a coward, a poor leader for Judah.

Nehemiah's response addressed both aspects to disgrace him. First, he says, "Should such a man as I flee" (v. 11)? In other words, "I'm a leader, a man of boldness and responsibility. How can I run away in times of danger? This would be inconsistent with my personality and responsibility." Second, he says, "And who is there such as I who will go into the temple to save his life" (v. 11)? "I'm a commander, a lay person, I am not a priest. I cannot go into the temple to save my life." Curiously, only after Nehemiah rejected the false prophecy, did Nehemiah "perceive that God had not sent him at all, but that he pronounced this prophecy against me because Tobiah and Sanballat had hired him" (v. 12). Undoubtedly, they had hoped that fear would motivate Nehemiah to "sin" by entering the temple (v. 13) thus disgracing himself publicly. The passage closes with a prayer that mentions other "prophets" who were collaborating with Tobiah and Sanballat (v. 14).

The attempt to trick Nehemiah through false prophecy failed, not because he immediately saw through deception. Nehemiah rejected the suggestion on the basis of his own identity: on the basis of who he was and who he was not. Nehemiah responded by pointing to his character and to his role as a leader. Timidity did not fit Nehemiah's identity, nor did an overriding self-interest. Yet, Nehemiah knew the limits of his personal magnitude. He was not a priest. Therefore, he could not enter the temple, even to save his life. We will best be able to discern when we know who we are. Remember our identity in Christ, and at the same time, never become too sure of ourselves.

Completion of the Wall – Nehemiah 6:15-16

One might expect that the completion of the wall would have received more fanfare in the text. Given what follows in Chapters 8-12, the book of Nehemiah clarifies that the wall itself is not the point. Regardless of how important it was, the wall only provided a secure environment for what really mattered: the covenant people of God living righteously as God's people.

One More Attack – Nehemiah 6:17-19

Though some who supported Nehemiah's leadership tried diplomatic efforts, Tobiah was not interested. The one thing that both Nehemiah and Tobiah could agree on was that they were opposed to each other. Internal alliances would keep feeding Tobiah with information. They were traitors to their nation, proving that blood is thicker than water. They should have put God first.

In summation we can conclude that in the Kingdom of God there will always be opposition. When confronted with personal attacks remember:

- When the enemy tries to distract you – stay focused – know your priorities.
- When the enemy tries to libel you – dismiss the charges and pray for strength. Trust in truth.
- When the enemy tries to disgrace you – know who you are and who you are not.

"So the wall was finished" (Neh. 6:15). But this marks a new beginning, for now Nehemiah must protect what he has accomplished. The walls and gates are built. Now it's time to focus on the community.

Concluding Thoughts

Nehemiah followed principles essential to maintain integrity as a community organizer and pastor. As a leader of the people, I cannot ask them to do anything that I am not willing to do myself. Whether you are a pastor of a church or a leader in your community's organization, you must work alongside the people and observably undertake the most difficult and risky aspects of that work. Nehemiah did not just organize and supervise; he picked up mallet and chisel and went to work on the wall. So should we (especially those of us who are pastors).

Second, it is imperative that you do not profit unjustly from your leadership in the community organization. Even the slightest hint of profiteering compromises the integrity of your work and allows others to question your motives. Nehemiah did not financially profit by his effort to rebuild the wall of Jerusalem; in fact, he spent more of his personal resources than he was paid as governor of Palestine. He had opportunity to lend with interest and did not. He had opportunity to speculate on land and profit from the restoration and did not. When he returned to the Persian court, he went back a poorer man (financially) than when he left. What Nehemiah did was invest his life and resources for the sake of the community.

This does not mean that a laborer is not worthy of his hire. He is. In fact the Bible says that those who labor in the Word and doctrine are worthy of double honor (1 Tim. 5:17-18). So the issue is not the ability to receive just compensation for service but what is the motivation of our hearts. And, how responsible have we been to invest what had been entrusted to us for the good of the community and the building of the Kingdom of God.

A community organization has great potential. It also has great capacity to do evil. Whenever people gain power, they can use that power for self-aggrandizement. The poor are no less likely to do this than are the rich, for the poor are subject to the same temptations as are the powerful. But if God's people – the church – have really entered into the life of the community, if they have identified with the people and worked side by side with them in the cause of justice and are willing to undertake the most difficult and risky aspects of that work, if the church and its people give themselves away rather than profit from their involvement, then the church gains a profound credibility in that community. Because of its integrity, its willingness to risk, its freedom to ask the hard questions, and its lack of self-interest, the church can become the conscience both of that organization and of the community. It can become the body that most shapes the spiritual grounding of the empowering effort.

It goes even further than that, however. The church that has undertaken that kind of incarnational ministry and has placed itself on the line with the poor is a church that gains profound respect in that community. In being willing to lose its life, it saves it. The community will know that the church did not have to risk its existence by joining in common cause with them. But it did risk, it did join, it did so work. In return, the people will want to know what motivated the church to commit itself thus to the people. They will want to hear about a Christ who also incarnated Himself in our world, and they will often respond to that Christ. That is why, today throughout the world, the city churches, which most uniformly experience growth, are churches that are involved intensely in community organizations.

Confront the people responsible; condemn their actions but not them as persons; expect them to mend their ways; participate in the recognition that all face the same temptation, work alongside the people, and do not intentionally profit by your own participation – these are the lessons Nehemiah teaches us on dealing with the internal injustice among the poor and marginalized, the people with whom we are working for their empowerment.

Discussion Questions

1. What opposition did Nehemiah face in this chapter?
2. When external and internal forces don't get the best of you the enemy will attack personally. How might you be prepared to be able to discern his tactic?
3. What proactive things can you do to be strengthened and prepared? What did Paul instruct in Eph. 6?
4. How does having a solid foundation in the Word of God help you discern when others try to divert you through some supposed spiritual means?
5. How can you be both confident and humble?
6. How does persistent work in God's strength silence the enemy?

CHAPTER 7
BROADING COMMUNITY INFLUENCE

The walls were completed, the gates restored, and the enemy was chagrined, but Nehemiah's work was not finished by any means. Now he had to practice the truth Paul emphasized in Ephesians 6:13, "And having done all, to stand." Nehemiah had been steadfast in building the walls and resisting the enemy, and now he had to be steadfast in consolidating and conserving the gains. "Look to yourselves," warned the Apostle John, "that we lose not those things which we have wrought, but that we receive a full reward" (2 John 8).

A city is much more than walls, gates, and houses; a city is people. The real problem was not the walls. The walls were simply Jerusalem's most immediate and urgent problem. The walls were now built. But if the Jerusalem community were truly to have a future, it would have to move from dealing with the lesser problem to the greater. The people had now proven to themselves that they were capable of such a mighty work as rebuilding a city's walls. Could they be equal to an even greater task – rebuilding the life of Jerusalem?

> Nehemiah 7:4 (NKJV)
> [4] Now the city *was* large and spacious, but the people in it *were* few, and the houses *were* not rebuilt.

How was Nehemiah going to rebuild the life of a nation? The essential problem of defeated, poor, or marginalized people is that they believe they are incapable of coping with the world. They accept and believe internally all the lies the systems and the people served by the systems tell them. They believe they are inferior.

Sociologists are fond of talking about a "culture of poverty." What they mean by that phrase is that poverty is not simply an absence of money or a lack of daily sustenance. Nor for marginalized people is the problem simply that society has, in some way, set them aside. The problem is that the poor perceive themselves as adequate only to be poor, and the marginalized believe they somehow deserve their marginalization. The people and systems that matter in life resign them to their poverty, their powerlessness, and their rejection.

This is why the Gospel is such "good news to the poor." The Gospel says to the poor, "You do matter! You are important! You are important enough for God to have provided for your salvation. You are important enough for Christ to have died for you. *You are somebody!*"

When a community is beaten by life, it too adopts a "culture of poverty." It may have adequate monies to function, but it is dysfunctional because it believes it deserves no better. Each of us can remember countless city neighborhoods into which we have entered where that sense of depression and resignation is so palpable that we can almost reach out and touch it. The issue is this: how can a community convinced it is unacceptable learn both to accept itself and to reformulate its own existence into a corporate life that is meaningful and full of hope? And what is the role of God's people, the church, in the transformation of such a depressed community? This was the issue Nehemiah faced upon the completion of Jerusalem's walls.

Organizing the Community

In the first half of the Book of Nehemiah, the people existed for the walls, but now the walls must exist for the people. It was time to organize the community so that the citizens could enjoy the quality of life God wanted them to have. God had great things in store for Jerusalem, for one day His Son would walk the city streets, teach in the temple, and die outside the city walls.

Chapter 7 of Nehemiah records three important steps that must be taken by any leader in order to protect the people and the work that had been done: enlisting leadership (Neh. 7:1-3); establishing citizenship (Neh. 7:4-69); and encouraging worship (Neh. 7:70-73).

Enlisting Leadership – Nehemiah 7:1-3

Like all good leaders, Nehemiah knew he couldn't do the job alone. One of his first official acts was to appoint two assistants, his brother Hanani (see Neh. 1:2) and Hananiah, who was in charge of the citadel. Why was Nehemiah convinced that these men would be good leaders? They had two wonderful qualities: they were faithful to God and they feared God. The greatest ability is dependability. The Apostle Paul instructed Timothy, "these things that you have heard from me among many witnesses, commit these to faithful men who will be able to teach others also" (2 Tim. 2:2). If we truly fear the Lord, we will be faithful to do the work He has called us to do. If we fear people instead of fearing God, we will end up getting trapped (Prov. 29:25); and that will lead to failure. God is looking for faithful men and women, who will have the courage and conviction to serve Him, come what may.

Gatekeepers were also appointed. What good are strong new gates if nobody is guarding them and controlling who enters and leaves the city? What good are walls if the gates are open to every foe that wants to enter the city? I understand that the *enemy penetrated the Great Wall of China* at least four times, and each time the guards were bribed. Gates and walls are only as good as the people who guard them. The gatekeepers were given specific instruction as to when to open and close the gates (Neh. 7:3). To open the gates early in the morning would only invite the enemy to come in while the city was asleep and unprepared. To close and lock the gates without the guards on duty might give the enemy agents opportunity to slip in unnoticed.

Nehemiah appointed two kinds of guards ("watches" v. 3): those to patrol the walls at specific stations and those to keep watch near their own houses. Since many of the people had worked on areas of the wall near their homes (3:10, 23, 28-30), Nehemiah now challenged them to guard the areas they had built. With guards at the gates, watchmen on the walls, and a solid "neighborhood watch," the city was safe from the outside attack.

All of this has a message for us today. If God's people don't protect what they have accomplished for the Lord, the enemy will come in and take over. Paul's admonition must be heeded: "And having done all, to stand" (Eph. 6:13). What a tragedy that prominent schools that once were true to the faith are today denying the faith, and churches that once preached the Gospel now have in their pulpits ministers who preach "another gospel."

Every Christian ministry is one short generation away from destruction, and God's people must be on guard. We need guards at the gates, faithful men and women who will not allow false Christians to get in and take over the ministry (2 Cor. 11:13-15). We need watchers on the walls to warn us when the enemy is approaching.

Christian parents need to guard their homes lest the enemy gets in and captures their children. When we become too comfortable with the enemy, we lack discernment of his devices. It is while God's servants are asleep and overconfident that the enemy comes in and plants his counterfeits (Matt. 13:25), so we must be awake and alert.

In this day when "pluralism" is interpreted by most people to mean "agree with everybody about everything and don't make any waves," Christians need to remember that they are different and must test everything by the Word of God. There are many religions, but there is still "no other name under heaven given among men, whereby we must be saved" (Acts 4:12). Anything that changes that message or weakens our motivation to get that message out is of the devil and must be opposed. We need guards at the gates and watchers on the wall, or the enemy will take over.

Establishing Citizenship – Nehemiah 7:4-69

Reading this long list of difficult names might be boring to the modern student, but these people were God's "bridge" from the defeats of the past to the hopes of the future. These Jews were the "living link" that connected the historic past with the prophetic future and made it possible for Jesus Christ to come into the world. Ezra 2 and Nehemiah 7 are to the Old Testament what Hebrews 11 is to the New Testament: a listing of the people whose faith and courage made things happen.

The structure of this list reveals fundamental values in the Jewish community. It shows the centrality of the temple. The priest, Levites and others who worked in the temple receive special mention. The list shows the importance of an individual's place of birth. A significant group of people is known by their city of origin rather than by their family origin. The list displays how much Israel valued ancestry. Those who could prove their genealogical roots belonged in the community; they had a place in the restored nation. This was not true of those who could not identify their family backgrounds. Both people and priest were affected. Priests were excluded from the priesthood.

Our modern cities are ethnic "melting pots", but in Jerusalem at that time, the important thing was to be a Jew and be able to prove your ancestry. Genealogies were "lifelines" that linked the Jews not only to the heritage of the past but also to their hope for the future. Not to be able to prove your ancestry meant second-class citizenship and separation from all God had given to Israel (Rom. 9:4-5).

There were ten different groups listed here, starting with the leaders who returned with Zerubbabel (Neh. 7:7), various families or clans (v. 8-25), priests (7:39-42), Levites (v. 43), temple singers (v. 44), gatekeepers (v. 45), various temple servants (v. 46-60), "Solomon's servants" (v. 57), priests who could not prove genealogies (v. 61-65), miscellaneous assembly (v. 67). The important thing here is not to count the people but to realize that these people counted. In leaving Babylon, they did much more than put their names on a list. They laid their lives on the altar and risked everything to obey the Lord and restore the Jewish nation. They were "pioneers of faith" who trusted God to enable them to do the impossible.

Categorizing those with indeterminate ancestry and excluding priests with this problem grates our notion of inclusivity. God's covenant with Abraham includes the blessing of his descendants (Gen. 12:2). Intermixing pure Jewish stock with pagan families consistently had led Israel into serious trouble. Every time they compromised the sacredness of ancestry, God's people quickly compromised the holiness of their religion. In this light, we can understand why a people who were seeking to be restored to God would want to be ethnically pure.

What is good for the people is also good for the ministers. The exclusion of priest as "defiled" seems particularly mean-spirited. But we must remember that the priesthood was hereditary. Only the descendents of Aaron were to serve as priest. If purported, priests could not demonstrate their family background, then they could very well be imposters. The people who had suffered through years of exile would be particularly sensitive to anything that might endanger their national renewal. At this strategic time of restoration, Israel needed priests that conformed to God's exact standard, so the questionable priests were excluded.

The list in Nehemiah 7 shows who rightly belonged to the restored community and who did not belong. It registers who is counted in and who is counted out. While all desire to be counted in, to belong to a group, we hate feeling excluded. Do you know the feeling? Have you ever felt like a fifth-wheel at a party or in a group of exclusive friends? Have you ever been the victim of prejudice because of your race or your gender? If you have ever felt the sting of exclusion, then you will be particularly sensitive to those Jews in our story who could not prove their parentage.

Before we point a self-righteous finger at anyone, consider that as Christians, we affirm that membership in the Body of Christ depends simply upon faith in Jesus Christ as Lord and Savior. We also accept our calling to draw outsiders to Christ by welcoming them into our gatherings. But our attitudes and actions often contradict these theological convictions.

Before we leave this section, it might be good for you to ask yourself, "If I had to prove my genealogy in order to get into God's city, could I do it?" You are headed for one of two destinies – heaven or hell – and only those who belong to God's family can enter heaven. You enter God's family by receiving Jesus Christ as your Savior, and this alone guarantees your entrance into heaven (John 1:11-12; 3:16; 14:6).

Encouraging Worship – Nehemiah 7:70-73

Citizens and leadership together can make a state, but it takes worship to make a state a godly nation. John Stuart Mill wrote, "The worth of a state, in the long run, is the worth of the individual composing it." But the worth of the individual depends on his or her relationship to God, and this involves worship. If individual godliness declines, the morality of the nation declines.

It was now the seventh month (Oct. – Nov.), when Israel was expected to celebrate the Feast of Trumpets, the Day of Atonement, and the Feast of Tabernacles (Lev. 23:23-44). There could have been no better time for Nehemiah to call the people together to honor the Word of God, confess their sins, and dedicate themselves and their work to the Lord. What began with *concern* (Neh. 1) led to *construction* (Neh. 2-3) and *conflict* (Neh. 4-7); and now it was time for *consecration* (Neh. 8-12).

As we serve the Lord, we must always do our best, but without His help and blessing, even our best work will never last. "Unless the Lord builds the house, they labor in vain who build it; unless the Lord guards the city, the watchman stays awake in vain" (Psalm 127:1). Nehemiah knew that there was a desperate need for the people to come back to the Lord and turn away from their secret sins that were grieving Him. Even though Nehemiah was the official representative of a pagan king, he did everything he could to glorify the God of Israel.

Key Lessons

One of the key lessons of this chapter is that people are important to God. When God wanted to take the next step in His great plan of redemption, He called a group of Jews to leave the place of exile and return to their own land. He gave them encouragement from the prophets and leadership from the people who feared God and wanted to honor Him. The Lord didn't send a band of angels to do the job; He used common people who were willing to risk their futures on the promises of God.

Today, God is still calling people to leave their personal "Babylons" to follow Him by faith. The church is living in a day of reproach (Neh. 2:17), and there are "ruins" all around us that need to be rebuilt. "If the foundations be destroyed, what can the righteous do?" David asked (Psalm 11:3). The answer is plain: the righteous can rebuild what has been torn down and start over again. If you think that an enemy victory is final, then you have lost your faith in God's promises. There is always a new beginning for those who are willing to pay the price.

This chapter reminds us that God keeps accounts of His servants. He knows where we came from, what family we belong to, how much we gave, and how much we did for Him. When we stand before the Lord, we will have to give an accounting for our lives before we can receive our rewards (Rom. 14:7-12); and we want to be able to give a good account.

The third lesson we must learn is that the Lord is able to keep His work going. The first group of Jewish exiles left Babylon for Judea in 538 B. C. And in spite of many difficulties and delays, rebuilt the temple and restored the worship. Eighty years later, Ezra and another group returned, and fourteen years after that, Nehemiah arrived and rebuilt the walls and gates.

During the days of Zerubbabel, God raised up the Prophets Haggai and Zechariah to give God's message to His people. No matter how discouraging the situation might be, God is able to accomplish His purpose if we will trust Him and do His will. John

Wesley was right when he said that God buries His workers but continues His work. We must not be discouraged!

Finally, and most important, we must all be sure that we know we are in the family of God. No matter how much they argued or protested, the priest without legitimate genealogies could not enter the temple precincts and minister at the altar. God is not impressed with our first birth; what He wants is that we experience a second birth and become His children. If you are not certain of your spiritual genealogy, read John 3:1-8 and 1 John 5:9-13 and make sure that your name is written down in heaven (Luke 10:20).

Discussion Questions

1. What does it mean by "we must guard what we build"?
2. A city is more than walls – What was Nehemiah's strategy to repopulate Jerusalem?
3. How did Nehemiah organize the community to give it meaning and hope?
4. How might you apply these steps taken to a present day ministry? Be specific about a ministry that you are involved in or one you would like to initiate.

CHAPTER 8
PEOPLE OF THE BOOK

In order for there to be cultural transformation we need to have our minds renewed (Rom. 12:1-2). Nehemiah Chapter 8 challenges our complacent approach to the Bible and our tendency to associate God's law with grudging obedience. The completion of the wall now sets the stage for spiritual transformation. Now that God's people finally have adequate physical protection – it is time for spiritual rebuilding.

Reading and Understanding the Law
Nehemiah 8:1-8

In the seventh month, (late September), the people gathered ("as one man") in an open area near the "Water Gate." The Water Gate was on the east side of the city. It is interesting that this assembly was not held in the temple court, where the altar was the focal point, but at one of the centers of city life, the kind of place where God's wisdom pleads most urgently to be heard (Prov. 1:20; 8:1). The law itself insisted that its voice must not be confined to the sanctuary but heard in the house and the street (Deut. 6:7).

We are surprised to find here that Ezra now returns to the scene of events. Having brought "The Book of the Law of Moses", he began to read it. We do not know how much of the Torah Ezra read, but we do know that he read and expounded for six hours.

The gathered assembly included a variety of persons: men and women who could hear with understanding. Those children who were old enough to understand the law joined the assembly. The Bible, especially the Book of Deuteronomy, regularly includes children in religious education, highlighting their importance as persons of faith (Deut. 4:10; 11:19; 31:12-13; Psalms 34:11; 78:5-7).

When Ezra opened the Book of the Law, or more accurately when he unrolled the scroll, all the people stood as a gesture of respect. When Ezra blessed the Lord, the people rejoiced, "Amen, Amen", while lifting their hands. Then they bowed down and worshipped God "with their faces to the ground."

We can see how worship involves participation. We worship God with all of our heart (rejoicing), with all of our mind (understanding), and with all of our strength (obeying). Worship is more than an emotional high or experience. Worship is the giving of your entire life to the service of Christ, our Savior and King.

Ezra read the law 'from morning until midday" or about six hours. Throughout this extended period of time, "the ears of all the people were attentive to the Book of the Law" (v. 3). Can you picture any congregation of U. S. Christians standing for six hours while the preacher reads the Scriptures? The average attention span of most people today is 17 minutes. Why were the people able to listen for half a day? Their oral culture (before television and printing press) nourished well-developed listening skills. They obviously hungered to know the law of God.

Not only did Ezra read the Law, but also many Levites "helped the people to understand the law." Paragraph by paragraph – "gave the sense." They helped the listener gain understanding. They helped them understand in their own language. The Parable of the Sower (Matt. 13:1-9, 18-23) emphasizes understanding the Word.

The Response of the People – Nehemiah 8:9-12

When the people heard and understood the law, they began to weep (v. 9). Perhaps they were convicted of sin. Perhaps they realized that their sufferings could have been prevented if they or their ancestors had obeyed God's precepts. Whatever the reason and though it seemed to be an appropriate response, the leaders rebuked the people for their tears: "This day is holy to the Lord your God; do not mourn or weep (v. 9). Instead, they encouraged the people to celebrate and to throw a great party. Those who did not have food appropriate for a party where to be invited anyway. Everyone was to celebrate and rejoice (Jer. 15:16; Psalm 19:8; 119:111). Weeping in response to the law will be encouraged later in Chapter 9, but rejoicing comes first. Faith based on God's Word will produce joy that will weather the storms of life.

Verses 1-12 not only emphasized an understanding of the law, but also identified this understanding as the cause for the joyful celebration. It isn't enough for us to read the Word or receive the Word as others expound it; we must also rejoice in the Word (Psalm 119:162; 112:1; 1:2).

The Feast of Booths – Nehemiah 8:14-18

Once again, in the desire "to understand the law, the leaders of Judah gathered to hear from Ezra." This time they learned about the Feast of Booths (Lev. 23:34-43). This feast begins on the 15th day of the 7th month (in early fall, Lev. 23:34). It includes days of rest, special offerings, feasting on newly harvested fruits, and living in booths for 7 days. By living in temporary structures of bush and sticks, the Israelites remembered the sojourning of their ancestors in the wilderness (Lev. 23:43). It sounds like an ancient version of church family camp.

Obligation and appreciation are certainly strong motives for serving the Lord, but celebration is even stronger. When we obey the Lord and serve Him because we rejoice in Him, then our service will be a delight and not drudgery. To the believer without joy, the will of God is punishment; but to the believer happy in the Lord, the will of God is nourishment (John 4:34).

When the leaders heard about the feast of booths, they called all Judah to participate in the festival (v. 15). It was a time of looking back to their days of wanderings. It was a time of looking around at the harvest and blessing from the hand of God. It was a time for looking ahead to the glorious kingdom God had promised His people Israel. For the first time in a long time, everyone was involved and the feeling of joy predominated.

The Importance of Understanding

The goal of understanding must be shared by those who teach and by those who learn. No matter how carefully one delivers a sermon – understanding requires effort on the part of the listeners. They must pay attention. In the process, one must engage both mind and heart. Unfortunately, many people who have gone to church for a lifetime have developed a habit of turning off their minds in church. We are responsible to worship God actively – that includes thinking energetically and participating completely. The mind grows by taking in. The heart grows by giving out.

This passage also suggests that complete education requires a setting that allows for interaction between teacher and student for questions and answers, discussion and personal engagement. Note that it required a team of Levites to reach the people in smaller groups. This speaks of our need to receive from each other. Also each home can continue to bring understanding to God's Word.

The Results of Understanding

Understanding is not the culmination of hearing God's truth. When the people grasped the sense of the law, they responded both emotionally and behaviorally. They wept and they rejoiced. Comprehensive communication of God's truth fosters a mental change that leads to transformation of the heart and lifestyle. It is a tragedy to spend a lifetime of Christian learning having our minds informed, but our hearts not touched. God's Word is not an educational elective but rather a life-transformation requirement.

We must know Christ and have His power recreate our lives. His power is the key! Life-transforming understanding occurs not only when the communicator and the learners have endeavored to teach and to learn, but when the Holy Spirit, by His power convicts, cleanses, heals, and transforms.

God's law leads not only to sorrow, but also to vibrant joy. When we fully understand the law, it's time to throw a party, because God gives the law, not to preclude our pleasure, but to maximize it. When God's truth affects our hearts and impacts our lives, then we will know fullness of joy.

At the dedication of Solomon's Temple there had been glory and beauty, natural and supernatural, to overwhelm the worshippers. In Nehemiah the focus, apart from a wooded platform, was a scroll – or more exactly, what was written in it. For the Jews this day was to prove to be a turning point. From now on, they would be predominately "the people of the book."

At the beginning of the Reformation period the pomp and circumstances of smells, bells, incense and nonsense was replaced by a cry for "Scripture Alone", a recommitment to God's Word.

If we are truly to be a people of restoration and reformation – we need to be people of the book. Simply put: We must understand the Word. We must rejoice in the Word. And we must obey the Word (Matt. 7:13-27).

Discussion Questions

1. Why is the Word of God the foundation for all true societies?
2. What does it mean "[the Levites] gave the sense, and helped them to understand the reading"?
3. What might be the results of understanding God's Word?
4. What did the reading of the Law prompt the people of Jerusalem to do?
5. There is a distinction between hearing and doing. What did Jesus say about this in Matthew 7? How can you apply this to your life and ministry?

CHAPTER 9
REMEMBERING OUR HERITAGE

Reflection is an integral part of the process needed for community transformation. Such reflection must include several strategic ingredients, which lead toward the reformation of the community's life. The first ingredient is a new and more liberated evaluation of the people's worth and capability, based upon their capacity to identify and deal with their corporate problems and to confront the systems and win. That is why community transformation cannot be addressed until the people are empowered as presented earlier. The people must have evidence that they are capable.

A second ingredient is a discovery and reinterpretation of the community's cultural heritage. As part of community rebuilding, the people need to celebrate their corporate past and to revise and integrate that heritage into the rebuilding process. A third ingredient is the people's social analysis of their culture. Through this process, the people are enabled to perceive how that society's systems have contributed to their malaise; this helps the people stop self-destructively minimizing or blaming themselves. A final ingredient is the people's recognition of their own complicity in their situation and, consequently, their own sinfulness, which is forgiven. As a result, God transforms their lives.

We see all of these ingredients present as Nehemiah helps the people deal with the substantive problem of rebuilding the life of Jerusalem (Neh. 8:1, 5-6, 10, 12, 18). After the people of Jerusalem rebuilt the wall, they had a party! What a party it was; it lasted for seven days! At that party, they read from the Book of the Law of Moses and praised God. They feasted, rejoiced, and played together.

The task facing Israel was a profound one, for the people had to shift from a commitment to rebuild the walls of Jerusalem to a realization that their real task was to rebuild the life of the community. Nehemiah began that shift through community celebration. He provided the opportunity for the people to celebrate the great work of their hands and the even greater work in their spirits – which occurred because of the work of their hands. Nehemiah orchestrated the victory within the context of reminding the people of their great heritage in being Israelites. They worshipped; they partied; they celebrated with great joy.

Community celebration is the best vehicle for enabling people to reflect substantively on their previous empowering actions and to discern the next risky – but necessary – steps for building community. Celebration gives permission to rejoice at what the people have accomplished, to congratulate and honor each other, to stand in solemn assembly together and reflect on what has happened, and to discern the next precarious steps the community needs to take in its interior transformation. When the community allows overt worship, celebration is the natural locus for recognizing the source of the community's strength and its potential in the God who calls it to enter the future with Him.

The church has celebration built into its life every week, at least it should! A community does not. Yet celebration is the single most effective activity for enabling a community to reflect on its just-completed actions and to move into the future. A primary responsibility of the community's organization, therefore, is to provide regular opportunities for the community to celebrate together. For it is its celebration which both demonstrates the depths of the community's potential and provides the incentive for next actions, which lead toward the transformation of that community.

Celebration of what the community has accomplished (and of God's blessings on that endeavor) is not sufficient to bring about that community's transformation. The second ingredient is the rediscovery of that community's cultural heritage. Note how that happened in Nehemiah's effort to reformulate the life of Israel in the following verses:

> Nehemiah 9:1 (NKJV)
> ¹ Now on the twenty-fourth day of this month the children of Israel were assembled with fasting, in sackcloth, and with dust on their heads.
>
> Nehemiah 9:5 (NKJV)
> ⁵ And the Levites, Jeshua, Kadmiel, Bani, Hashabniah, Sherebiah, Hodijah, Shebaniah, *and* Pethahiah, said: "Stand up *and* bless the LORD your God Forever and ever! "Blessed be Your glorious name, Which is exalted above all blessing and praise!
>
> Nehemiah 9:7 (NKJV)
> ⁷ "You *are* the LORD God, Who chose Abram, And brought him out of Ur of the Chaldeans, And gave him the name Abraham;
>
> Nehemiah 9:9-10 (NKJV)
> ⁹ "You saw the affliction of our fathers in Egypt, And heard their cry by the Red Sea. ¹⁰ You showed signs and wonders against Pharaoh, Against all his servants, And against all the people of his land. For You knew that they acted proudly against them. So You made a name for Yourself, as *it is* this day.
>
> Nehemiah 9:13 (NKJV)
> ¹³ "You came down also on Mount Sinai, And spoke with them from heaven, And gave them just ordinances and true laws, Good statutes and commandments.

Nehemiah 9:22-23 (NKJV)
²² "Moreover You gave them kingdoms and nations, And divided them into districts. So they took possession of the land of Sihon, The land of the king of Heshbon, And the land of Og king of Bashan. ²³ You also multiplied their children as the stars of heaven, And brought them into the land Which You had told their fathers To go in and possess.

Nehemiah 9:25 (NKJV)
²⁵ And they took strong cities and a rich land, And possessed houses full of all goods, Cisterns *already* dug, vineyards, olive groves, And fruit trees in abundance. So they ate and were filled and grew fat, And delighted themselves in Your great goodness.

The people of Israel celebrated the work of their hands – the rebuilding of the wall of Jerusalem. Further, they celebrated their newfound communal strength and self-determination, along with the love and favor of God so obviously showered upon them. Finally, Israel recounted its history. The people remembered from whom they had come. They recited the events that shaped them into a great and glorious nation.

Why was it important for the Jews gathered in their rebuilt Jerusalem to recite their history? First, it reminded them of their great origins, their illustrious past. It said to them, "You have not always been a defeated, weak, and persecuted people. You were at one time a nation with which God made a covenant; you were miraculously delivered from Egyptian slavery as God humbled the mightiest ruler at that time; also you were chosen by God out of all the nations on the face of the earth and given a land – this land – that was then flowing with milk and honey. You were given a city – the city of Jerusalem – as the city in praise of God. All of this you were. And all of this you are, because the blood of your ancestors still courses through you. The commitment of God to your ancestors is a commitment that still resides with you. And as you are faithful, God will honor that covenant and will bless you, just as the Lord blessed your ancestors when they were obedient to Him."

Every community has a history; every people group moments of glory and honor. Reclaiming the history of a community and/or its people is essential for its transformation from defeated to self-determined. That is why the black history movement is vitally important to African-Americans. It reminds this people of color of their great heritage – of the great nations they built in Africa, the kings from which they are descended, the creativity and dignity with which they resisted the abasement of slavery, and the great contributions African-Americans of the past made in politics, government, economics, music, art, science, and religion in the United States. All of this is a way of saying, "We are somebody; look what great blood courses through our veins!"

The second reason for recounting the past is to demonstrate to the people that their ancestors overcame even greater obstacles than they now face. And "since we did it before, we can do it again!" Such recognition breed's self-confidence in a previously defeated people, convincing them that they can handle a task that, on the surface, seems overwhelming – even rebuilding the wall of Jerusalem!

In addition to celebrating the people's capacity for self-determination (demonstrated by successful organizing and taking action) and the community's cultural heritage, a third ingredient in community transformation is the social analysis, in order that they might understand why a people greatly loved by God could become powerless.

Nehemiah 9:36-37 (NKJV)
[36] "Here we *are,* servants today! And the land that You gave to our fathers, To eat its fruit and its bounty, Here we *are,* servants in it! [37] And it yields much increase to the kings You have set over us, Because of our sins; Also they have dominion over our bodies and our cattle At their pleasure; And we *are* in great distress.

The people of Israel were discontent. The worship of God, their celebration of the great "work of their hands" and the recital of their illustrious history have all worked to increase their discontent over their present pitiable state. Why do they live in such powerlessness, such deprivation? The reflection over their history shows them that it is not God's doing. Neither are they an incapable people, for both their history and their own recent action of rebuilding the wall demonstrates to them that they are capable of great things.

Why do they live in poverty and powerlessness? "We are slaves today ... in the land you gave our forefathers ... [Our] abundant harvest goes to kings ... [who] rule over our bodies and our cattle as they please." On reflection, the Jews of Jerusalem realized that they are weak and poor because the nation's political and economic systems are intentionally and purposefully arrayed against them to the benefit of those who run those systems. That is biblical social analysis!

This was a fact, that "kings ruled over them", but why? Through the understanding of Biblical analysis they could discern that the root issue was not those very kings, but their present oppression was due to the rebellion and disobedience of their ancestors to God. Aware of this sets the stage for transformation

Nehemiah 9:29-35 (NKJV)
^{29} And testified against them, That You might bring them back to Your law. Yet they acted proudly, And did not heed Your commandments, But sinned against Your judgments, 'Which if a man does, he shall live by them.' And they shrugged their shoulders, Stiffened their necks, And would not hear. ^{30} Yet for many years You had patience with them, And testified against them by Your Spirit in Your prophets. Yet they would not listen; Therefore You gave them into the hand of the peoples of the lands. ^{31} Nevertheless in Your great mercy You did not utterly consume them nor forsake them; For You *are* God, gracious and merciful. ^{32} "Now therefore, our God, The great, the mighty, and awesome

God, Who keeps covenant and mercy: Do not let all the trouble seem small before You That has come upon us, Our kings and our princes, Our priests and our prophets, Our fathers and on all Your people, From the days of the kings of Assyria until this day. [33] However You *are* just in all that has befallen us; For You have dealt faithfully, But we have done wickedly. [34] Neither our kings nor our princes, Our priests nor our fathers, Have kept Your law, Nor heeded Your commandments and Your testimonies, With which You testified against them. [35] For they have not served You in their kingdom, Or in the many good *things* that You gave them, Or in the large and rich land which You set before them; Nor did they turn from their wicked works.

The fourth ingredient of reflection, which leads to community transformation, is recognition of the community's and one's own culpability. Israel is not under Persian authority simply because the systems are arrayed against it. That is a significant part of the problem, but not the whole problem. Israel is under oppressive political and economic authority because of the irresponsible way God's chosen people choose to live and still choose to live. They have been their own worst enemy, and they have consequently contributed to their own malaise.

True community reformulation occurs when we admit to the evil within us, confess our own sins and our ancestor's sin in contributing to our bondage or marginalization, and throw ourselves upon the mercy and forgiveness of God. By God's grace we can be empowered and forgiven.

Confession may include a recital of God's nature, of His works, as well as statements of human sins. In both Hebrew and the Greek, confession includes the characteristic of telling the truth – the truth about God and the truth about one's own self. Confession then is telling the truth about God's glory and grace as well as man's ingratitude. Therefore, confession is worship, not mere wallowing in self-reproach. The confession in Nehemiah 9 contains a rich recounting of Biblical history from creation through the time of

Nehemiah. It begins with the recognition of the one Creator God (v. 6), moves through the covenant with Abraham (v. 7-8), on to the deliverance of the Exodus (v. 9-12) and finally narrates the Mosaic covenant and the establishment of the Law (v. 13-15). The remainder of the confession moves back and forth between the sin of the people and God's gracious but increasingly corrective response.

Notice particularly the elements that highlight God's faithful and forgiving nature, "But You are God ... ready to pardon ... gracious and merciful ... slow to anger ... abundant in kindness." Other elements of the confession echo well-known Biblical themes and phrases: "Their clothes did not wear out and their feet did not swell" (Neh. 9:21; Deut. 8:4). "So they took possession of the land of Sihon the land of the King of Heshbon, and the Land of Og, King of Bashanm" (Neh. 9:22; see Deut. 1:4; Joshua 2:10; Psalm 135:11). "When they cried to You, You heard from heaven; and according to Your abundant mercies, You gave them deliverers who served them" (Neh. 9:27; see Judges 2:18).

Verse 33 sums up the essence of the confession succinctly: "However, You are just in all that has befallen us; For You have dealt faithfully, But we have done wickedly." Although God had been patient, merciful, forgiving, and always faithful, the people of God had been rebellious, forgetful, sinful, and consistently faithless in their covenant relationship with Him.

This explains the discomforting condition of Judah in the day of Nehemiah (Neh. 9:36-37). The people of God were reaping what they had sown. And often individuals and communities reap what has been previously sown, or has been sown into them. They deserved their sentence to serve foreign kings. The confession of Chapter 9 offers no excuses – only an admission of the people's perpetual guilt in contrast to God's perpetual grace. The covenant of renewal stands not upon any confidence that the people have in themselves but upon God's continued and undying faithfulness.

In reflection we see the people gathered to tell the truth about themselves, and, more importantly, they told the truth about God. Usually, when we confess our sins we fail to tell the whole truth. We tend to separate "confession of faith" from "confession of sin."

Winston Churchill stated, "Men occasionally stumble over the truth, but most of them pick themselves up and hurry off as if nothing happened." Jesus said, "And this is the condemnation, the Light is come into the world, and men loved darkness rather than light, because their deeds were evil" (John 3:19). Our tendency as fallen people is to reject what is true in favor of what is comfortable and to choose what is familiar over what is right (2 Tim. 4:3-4). We would be better to imitate the people of Nehemiah 9.

Telling the whole truth highlights the nature of sin. Our society minimizes sin. The efforts to understand our actions, to look for causes, and to identify compulsions are not necessarily wrong. Psychology and sociology have their place. But we Christians have developed a particular skill in minimizing our sin by comparing ourselves with others. Yet all of our efforts to dilute sin dissipate in the presence of our Holy, Righteous God. As long as we compare ourselves with others, we can play this self-justification game. But when we place our sins alongside the attributes and actions of God, feeble excuses to discount our wickedness fail miserably. Only when we see ourselves as we truly are – sinners, lost without God – will our hearts be genuinely open for healing, forgiveness and profound cleansing. By confessing both who we are and who God is, we lay the groundwork for spiritual restoration.

Telling the whole truth encourages us to confess our sin. By confessing the faithfulness of God, while confessing our sin, we discover greater freedom to tell the truth about ourselves. Aware of the grace of God that justifies us, we are made aware of our responsibility and empowered for action.

Our repentance is merely the outcome of our personal realization of the Atonement, which God has worked out for us. The Apostle Paul put it this way in writing to the Romans: "God demonstrates His own love toward us, in that while we were still sinners, Christ died for us" (Rom. 5:8). This stands at the center of the whole truth about God.

Secular community organizations rarely reach this community-transforming place because it has difficulty turning to God for forgiveness for the people's sinful contribution to their own disenfranchisement. To turn to God would be to cease being a secular organization; it would mean admitting to the spiritual dimensions of a community's and a city's bondage. Thus the empowerment work of the church in the city is strategic, because only the church can deal with sin and salvation in relation to both the deterioration and the transformation of a community. This is the particularly godly contribution the church can make to the empowerment of the marginalized and defeated people of the city.

It should be noted how late in the empowerment process one's own complicity is introduced. An essential problem of powerless people is their quickness to blame themselves for all that happened to them. To raise the issue too quickly is to defeat the entire empowerment process. This is so because, recognizing one's own culpability, a powerless person will only retreat into self-blame and the blaming of the poor around him. However, once a community has moved into participation in a coalition around the issues, has tasted a series of victories when dealing with the issues, has participated in considerable social analysis, and has dealt successfully with conflict, that community is ready to look at its own contribution to its bondage or marginalization. It has gained enough self-respect and dignity of character that its people can tolerate reflection upon their corporate and individual culpability. Because the people now have more self-confidence, they can look frankly and openly at their own sin and not be devastated or immobilized by it.

Discussion Questions

1. How does reading God's Word help you to discern our present state?
2. As a result of hearing God's Word, how did the Jews respond?
3. How does recounting your history help you to have a proper vision for the future? What other benefits does it give you?
4. How does reflection lead to empowerment?

CHAPTER 10
BUILDING THROUGH COVENANT

In a certain church, there was a man who always ended his prayers with, "And, Lord, clean the cobwebs out of my life! Clean the cobwebs out of my life!" One of the members of the church began to be weary of hearing this same insincere request week after week, because he saw no change in the petitioner's life. So, the next time he heard the man pray, "Lord, clean the cobwebs out of my life!" He interrupted with, "And while you're at it, Lord, *kill the spider!*"

It is one thing to offer the Lord a passionate prayer of confession; such as we have in Nehemiah chapter 9, and quite something else, to live an obedient life after we say "Amen." But the people in the assembly were serious about their praying and were determined, by God's grace, to make a new beginning and live to please the Lord.

The leaders of Israel did not make "a sure covenant" with God because of their sin, or in order to earn God's approval. Rather, they made the covenant on the basis of God's grace – in response to His mercy. In reality, the people did not make a covenant at all. The Bible regularly describes God as the One who makes covenants with people; only rarely are people said to make covenant with God. In chapter 10, the Israelites did not make a covenant with God; rather they make a firm agreement to live according to the former covenant that God had established through Moses (Neh. 10:29). This leads us to the theological truth that: God is the covenant maker; His people are the covenant renewers.

The priest, Levites, and secular leaders who sealed the covenant took a stand for God, much as the signers of the Declaration of Independence took a stand for political freedom in the United States over 200 years ago. They led by costly example, not by coercion. The text of 10:28 clarifies that those who "signed on" with the leaders did so on the basis of their "knowledge and understanding." This extended not only to heads of families, but "to their wives, sons, and their daughters" (v. 28). Even in this solidly patriarchal society, each person had to make his or her own choice to support the firm commitment of the leaders.

We who lead today would do well to consider how faithfully we imitate this example. Do we lead our people by living exemplary lives and taking stands according to our convictions? Or do we coerce and compel those who follow us to do what we want them to do? Are we helping our people to grow as mature decision makers, or do we keep them in moral infancy by treating them as immature children?

The "rest of the people" (v. 28) joined with "the nobles" by entering into "a curse and an oath to walk in God's law" (v. 29). The language of curses and oaths sounds strange to modern ears. Notice that they not only swore to walk obediently, they also swore to be punished if they failed to walk obediently. This is what it means to enter a curse. Often covenants, including those between God and people, had curses associated with them (see Deut. 28:22). Even with unspecified curses, however, the people chose to join with their leaders in making a new commitment to God. They agreed to "walk in God's law ... and to observe and do all the commandments of the Lord our Lord and His ordinances and His statutes" (v. 29).

Special Tenets of the Firm Agreement
Nehemiah 10:30-39

The people promised to obey all of God's law (v. 29). In addition, they made specific promises concerning: intermarriage (v. 30), the Sabbath (v. 31) and support for the temple and its personnel

(v. 32-39). Some specific tenets of these promises simply restate Biblical laws, for example; bringing "the first fruits of the ground" (Neh. 10:35). But most extend or reinterpret Biblical precedents. For example; bringing "the first fruits of all fruit of all trees" went beyond the requirements of the law.

The law needed to be extended because the life setting of God's people had changed since the time God originally gave the law. Verse 31 provides an apt illustration. The Ten Commandments stated clearly that one should not work on the Sabbath (Exod. 20:8-10). Therefore, the Israelites refrained from selling anything on the Sabbath.

But between the giving of the law and the time of Nehemiah, the situations of God's people had changed. Foreigners had come to live within Judah who had no reservations about selling and buying goods on the Sabbath (Neh. 13:16). So the question arose: In light of the Sabbatical Law, could Jews buy on the Sabbath? Verse 31 answers the question negatively: Neither selling anything nor buying on the Sabbath was acceptable. So the people instituted an ancient version of "Blue Laws" prohibiting commerce on the Sabbath.

Thus, the special promises contained in this agreement reflect the issues and crises of Nehemiah's day. These included: The problem of intermarriage with "the peoples of the land," indebtedness, and inadequate support for the temple and its ministry. Given the likelihood that Malachi prophesied around the time of Nehemiah, we have another witness to the people's utter failure to provide acceptable tithes and offerings to God (Mal. 1:7-8; 12-14; 3:8-10). Verse 39 sums up the majority of the tenets simply: "We will not neglect the House of our God."

Reflections on Nehemiah 9:38-10-39

First, like the people of Israel in Nehemiah 10, we must apply God's permanent standards to a world that is in constant transformation. Secondly, as the people of God we must renew our commitment to God's covenant (Jer. 31:31-34). Jesus became the mediator of the New Covenant through His death (Heb. 9:15;

12:24). We who believe in Him have become the new covenant people of God.

God promised that in the New Covenant we would know Him intimately. Do you know God intimately? Do you enjoy spending time with Him? Do you live in true fellowship with Christ? Are you experiencing the New Covenant offered through the blood of Jesus?

Perhaps you find the need for several types of covenant renewal such as a daily recommitment of your life to Christ, a declaration each day saying, "Lord, I belong to You – use me this day for Your purpose and glory." Additionally, a weekly renewal may be chosen, one that comes through worship – joining brothers and sisters as together you affirm your faith in song, confession and in prayer. Beyond that, your faith journey is marked by certain watershed events in which you can renew your covenant relationship with God in a profound way, each time you are confronted with the opportunity to surrender even more of yourself to God, to live renewed within His covenant of grace.

A word of caution must be addressed here. Whenever we consider our covenant with God, we run the risk of trying to earn His grace. We will be tempted to say: "If I can only get my life together, then I'll be acceptable to God." "If I can only be good enough, then God will love me." But Nehemiah and the people knew that such arrogance only turned to folly. In their confession of sin, the people remembered with excruciating detail how they had broken their covenant with God. The covenant renewal of Nehemiah 10 is not an attempt to earn back God's favor; it is a response, in gratitude, to His favor already given.

Whenever we renew our covenantal relationship with God, we do so because God's spirit has drawn us, for our very desire for renewal comes from the Holy Spirit. Renewing our relationship with Christ no longer grows out of a youthful idealism. We no longer believe we can be pretty good Christians. Now, when we renew our faith in Christ, we know all too well our past failures and our penchant to fail again. Renewal comes from God's grace in our life, and we look ahead with certainty to the times when we will, once again, need to depend on more of God's grace.

Community Action

Community transformation actually occurs when the people move beyond reflection to an intentional and even more difficult action. The stepping-stones mentioned previously will lead toward community transformation, but only the intentional corporate action of the individuals of that community will lead to community reformulation. Chapter 10 of Nehemiah tells what the people of Israel decide together to do in order to rebuild the life of Jerusalem and of the nation (see Neh. 10:28-29).

In order to rebuild the life of Jerusalem – to transform the community – the people determined together to obey a discipline that included not marrying Gentiles, not trading with Gentiles on the Sabbath, canceling all debts every seven years, supporting the temple through an annual tithe of their income and goods, contributing time each year to work in or for the temple, and even contributing their firstborn sons for temple service (Neh. 10:30-39).

Such a plan of action would be repressive except for one factor. The people set this discipline. There is no evidence in the text of Nehemiah's participation in or leadership of the process at all. This plan of action was initiated by an act of the people responding to the revealed Word of God.

An essential ingredient of the community's action must be participatory decision-making. The people of the community have been powerless precisely because of the city's political and economic (and perhaps even religious) systems. From the very origins of the community organization – when coalitions are pulled together around issues identified by the people – it must be the people (and not the organizer nor the church) who must determine the actions the coalitions will take to address these issues. As the organization moves from issue-identification to reflection and action and the confrontation of the city's systems and structures, each decision on community objectives, strategies, and tactics must be made in a participatory manner. As the community's organization moves into the reformulation of the life of the community, shared decision-making becomes of even greater importance. The more difficult and demanding the decisions of an oppressed community become, the more it needs to arrive at those decisions through participatory democracy.

We see the Jewish community moving from a decision of what to do to the act of doing it. Nehemiah writes of the symbolic action the people took to validate their decision: "And because of all this, we make a sure covenant and write it; our leaders, our Levites, and our priests seal it" (Neh. 9:38).

Once the people have decided together what they need to do in order to rebuild the life of the nation and of its city, they symbolize each person's participation in the implementation of that decision by publicly endorsing a binding agreement. It is as if the people, committed to the action they must undertake, ask, "Where do we sign?"

How do people move beyond networking, community organizing, and issue orientation to the full empowerment of a community? A truly transformed community is born out of community celebration, reflection, participatory decision-making, and intentional group action.

Another view of this is Acts 6, where the Apostles lay out the broad based guidelines and requirements for selecting deacons, but the people make recommendation/ selections in keeping with the guidelines established. This is a great example of leaders and the people participating together.

Discussion Questions

1. What is the purpose of a covenant? In order to walk in covenant relationship what must be present?
2. When God initiates a covenant, what is man's responsibility? In the renewal of the covenant with God what did the people of Israel affirm to do? How did their decisive action affect community transformation?

CHAPTER 11
MODELING PROPER GOVERNMENT

As the community empowering process matures, those who organized the process take on a changing role (see Ephesians 4:1-16). The people, having determined what must be done to build and sustain their newly emerging community, set about doing it. The people of the community who have naturally emerged as its leaders lead them. The people, through the community's organization, are now discerning and identifying the pivotal issues and problems of the community, developing objectives and strategies for addressing those issues, and taking action to implement those decisions.

Some of those actions may be substantive in nature and in effort, but the people will be capable of taking on such long-term and intensive activity. They will even be able to deal with occasional failures without it influencing the way they feel about themselves, their community, or their organization. Most rewarding of all is that the people sill set stricter requirements for the maintenance and development of their community than their leaders would dare set; these limits will be acceptable simply because it is the people who are setting them.

All of these signs of a community's maturation are evidenced in the closing chapters of the Book of Nehemiah. Chapter 11 tells how the people carried out the commitments they had made to each other and before God in chapter 10. They identified new problems. The most notable was that, even with the voluntary effort approved earlier by the community (Neh. 10:32-39), the city of Jerusalem was not being adequately populated. Therefore they came up with an ingenious measure (Neh. 11:1-2).

The Jews took the ancient biblical injunction of the tithe (Lev. 27:30-33; Deut. 14:22-29) and applied it to people. Israel had formerly given a tenth of its produce and its money to the temple each year. Now, Israel would contribute a tenth of all its families to Jerusalem, in order to repopulate it.

It was a decision of the people. The people, therefore, gladly accepted the lot to move to Jerusalem. One-tenth of the nation's families gathered up their households left the villages in which they had lived all their days, and moved their families into the city to establish a new life. This was massive disruption of a people, but the people did it willingly.

Those elected to remain in their villages "blessed" the ones who offered to move, presumably because it entailed considerable sacrifice. Verses 3-24 provide a categorical listing of those who settled in Jerusalem: "The children of Judah" (v. 4-6), "the sons of Benjamin" (v. 7-9), and "the priests" (v. 10-14), "the Levites" (v. 15-18) and others (v. 19-24). Every now and then the list adds an item of special interest. Some of the men were "valiant" (v. 6). There were "mighty men of valor" (v. 14). The "Nethinim" were given to the service of the sanctuary to assist the Levites. Also included were people with particular responsibilities (v. 21-24). Those who were not chosen by lot to live in Jerusalem settled in the surrounding villages.

God brought the remnant back home because He had a special job for them to do; and to abandon the restored city was to obstruct the working out of God's will through Israel. The Jews were asked to heed a call not unlike the one Paul wrote in Romans 12:1:

> "I beseech you therefore, brethren, by the mercies of God, that you present your bodies a living sacrifice, holy, acceptable to God, which is your reasonable service."

Never underestimate the importance of simply being physically present in the place where God wants you. Your consistent presence brings encouragement to others. You may not be asked to perform some dramatic ministry, but simply being there is a ministry. The men, women, and children who helped to populate the city of Jerusalem were serving God, their nation, and future generations by their steps of faith.

God uses many people with different gifts and skills to accomplish His work (see Rom. 12:1-8). The important thing is that we give our bodies to the Lord so that He can use us as His tools to accomplish His work. Each person is important and each task is significant.

Nehemiah listed other temple ministers (Neh. 12:1-26). He states that the king of Persia helped support the ministry of the temple (v. 23). Since the king wanted the Jewish people to pray for him and his family, he shared in the temple expenses (Ezra 6:8-10; 7:20-24). In our modern democracies, where there is confusion about the separation of church and state, this kind of support would be questioned. But the province of Judah was one small part of a great empire, ruled by an all-powerful king; and the king did for the Jews what he did for all other provinces. Christians today are commanded to pray for civil leaders (1 Tim. 2:1-2; see also Jer. 29:7), and this should be done daily and on each Lord's Day when the church assembles to worship.

Pethahiah (Neh. 12:24) was the king's agent who represented the Jews at court. People involved in government are God's ministers (Rom. 13:7), whether they realize it or not; and if they are faithful, they are serving the Lord just as much as the priests and Levites in the temple.

In Nehemiah 12:25-36, Nehemiah names the villages where the Jews were living, some of which were quite a distance from Jerusalem. When the exiles returned to the land of Babylon, they would naturally want to settle in their native towns and villages. They would still be under the authority of Nehemiah and expected to be loyal to the king of Persia. This loyalty to their native cities was what helped make it difficult for Nehemiah to recruit people to reside in Jerusalem. While it is good to cultivate local loyalties, we must remember that there are larger obligations that must be considered. The work of the Lord is bigger than any one persons ministry or the ministry of any one assembly.

The covenant renewal of chapter 10 precedes the list of chapters 11 and 12. According to Ezra – Nehemiah, renewal does not conflict with order, but rather, it leads to order. Presumably, a proper ordering of the settlers in Jerusalem and the organization of the temple ministry would prolong the renewal that began with the rebuilding of the temple and culminate in the signing of a firm agreement (Neh. 10).

Of course, order can squelch genuine renewal. Sometimes we embrace so much order that the Holy Spirit, who moves where He wills (John 3:8), has no room to move! This is not to say that spiritual freedom and order are enemies. In 1 Corinthians 12-14, Paul encourages the free exercise of spiritual gifts while at the same time He provides rules by which these gifts can operate "decently and in order" (1 Cor. 14:40).

Progressive Understanding of Balanced Government Structure

We find that in the Old and New Testaments, God develops progressively our understanding of balanced governmental structure. In the Old Testament, the benefits of a combined government of monarchy (government of the one), aristocracy (government of the few) and democracy (government of the many) is developed for us.

God called Moses to lead the children of Israel out of Egypt and form a new nation with Jehovah as King but with Moses governing the nation just like he was trained by education in Egypt. Jethro, his father-in-law, informed Moses that leading and governing the people by himself (monarchy) will cause both he and the people to wear away. The Bible clearly indicated the failure of monarchy as a system of government. That is why it was a step backwards for Israel to return to monarchy years later (1 Samuel 8) in rejection of God's government.

In the development of a godly structure we see a first step in expanding the leadership representation.

> Exodus 18:21 (NKJV)
> [21] Moreover you shall select from all the people able men, such as fear God, men of truth, hating covetousness; and place *such* over them *to be* rulers of thousands, rulers of hundreds, rulers of fifties, and rulers of tens.

Here we find representatives elected by the people instituted to represent the government of the many (Deut. 1:13). They were elected by the people and represented their needs in smaller groups of thousands, hundreds, fifties, and tens. This gave the nation of Israel over 78,000 elected leaders to help Moses govern over three million people. With 78,000 slaves ruling other slaves – no wonder they couldn't lead properly. The inmates were running the prison.

An interesting commentary can be followed with Israel now having a government representing God's vision (Moses) and the needs of the people (elected representatives of small units). When Moses went up into the mountain, God's vision seemed to go with him. With only a democratic government remaining, the elected leaders quickly pleased the people in forming a golden calf. This demonstrates for us the failure of a democracy. It will turn to Mobocracy and the lowest common denominator, setting the state for greater tyranny.

The complaining of the people through their representatives was so strong that Moses could not take it anymore. There was something missing that he needed in the government of this people. It seemed that the elected leaders always had the needs of the people in mind, and thus Moses was left alone to lead the nation according to God's vision and purpose. God had an answer for this:

> Numbers 11:14 (NKJV)
> [14] I am not able to bear all these people alone, because the burden *is* too heavy for me.

Numbers 11:16 (NKJV)

¹⁶ So the LORD said to Moses: "Gather to Me seventy men of the elders of Israel, whom you know to be the elders of the people and officers over them; bring them to the tabernacle of meeting, that they may stand there with you.

Added to the governmental structure was a senate, which was made up of 70 princes (12 leaders, one head from each tribe and 58 heads of the thousands). The actual word used for "prince" here is the word "senator". The people did not elect these individuals; they were taken from the elected. They came out of the elected groups of Elders and bore the burden with Moses, representing not the needs of the people, but the needs of the nation. In a sense they balanced the needs of the people with principle and direction for the whole.

Thus, a balanced structure of the one, few, and many was established here in the Old Testament. In later years, the judges fulfilled Moses role (after Joshua), yet time after time, the nation was perverted due to the lack of character in the people. As a result of not training the next generation (since no governmental structure is going to insure godliness), all of Israel changed their governmental structure to be like all other nations.

In the New Testament, we see some of the same principles in operation. Israel still had its external form of government when the New Testament opens. The Elders were the representatives. The Sanhedrin was the senate. And they had leaders that were recognized in Rome. Israel was a kind of nation within a nation in Rome.

The Sanhedrin is thought to have originated in the 3rd century B.C. Known as "The Great Council," it was believed to be founded and presided over by Ezra after the return from captivity. The Great Synagogue was an assembly of 120 members whose purpose was to arrange religious matters; their motto was "Set a Hedge About the Law". This formation was the forerunner of the Sanhedrin. The Sanhedrin consisted of at least 70 members: the High Priest as President, Chief Priests (the 24 courses of priests),

The Scribes or Lawyers (Interpreters of the Law) and the Elders-Representatives of the Laity.

The local synagogue in the various cities functioned in allegiance to the Sanhedrin. The local synagogue's services were presided over by a Chief or Rabbi, assisted by a Council of Elders. The main objective was not public worship but rather religious instruction from the law. These local synagogues could only teach the interpretations of the Law handed down from the Sanhedrin. When the Sanhedrin rejected Jesus as their Messiah, so did the local synagogues. In seeking to set a hedge about the Law, they determined to formulate an authoritative interpretation. While they guarded the Law to the letter, they also accumulated numerous traditions, which they placed alongside the Law. These traditions grew out of their desire to apply the Law to their ever-changing conditions of life. As this body of traditional interpretation grew, it became known as the "Oral Law", which through the centuries gained equal status with the "Written Law" in authority.

Jesus rebuked this group for making the Word of God of no effect through the tradition they handed down (Mark 7:13). In other words, their tradition superseded the Word of God therefore making the Word of God of less effect in their lives. Also, it helped them to indulge in their carnal ways in leadership and every way of life.

The Sanhedrin was made up of several sects. The Pharisees were one of the sects thought to have originated in the third century B.C. when under Greek domination there was a strong tendency among the Jews to accept Greek culture with its pagan religious customs. The rise of the Pharisees was a reaction to and protest against this tendency among their fellow-countrymen. Their aim was to preserve their national integrity and strict conformity to Mosaic Law. They later developed into self-righteous hypocritical formalists.

The sect of the Sadducees was thought to have originated about the same time as the Pharisees. They were guided by secular considerations. They were in favor of adopting Greek customs. A priestly clique, the Sadducees were the religious officials of their nation, though they were avowedly irreligious. They were not numerous, but they were wealthy and influential. To a great extent, they controlled the Sanhedrin, even though they were rationalistic and worldly-minded.

The Scribes were copiers of Scripture. It was a calling of early origin. Their business was to study and interpret as well as copy the Scriptures. Because of their minute acquaintance with the Law, they were also called lawyers and were recognized as authorities. The decisions of leading Scribes became the "Oral Law" or "Tradition". They were influential before the days of printing.

Jesus confronted the Pharisees, Sadducees and Scribes often for the hypocrisy (see Matt. 23:13-16, 23-30). These words of Jesus constitute a most bitter denunciation falling from His lips. Jesus demonstrated respect to sinners, publicans and the common people. Through every century, the church has been cursed with leaders similar to those described in the 23rd chapter of Matthew: irreligious professional religionist, parading themselves in holy garments, pompous fellows, self-important, strutting around like lords, preaching religion, yet having none.

The Apostle Paul warned Timothy about such things:

2 Timothy 2:1-5 (NKJV)
[1] You therefore, my son, be strong in the grace that is in Christ Jesus. [2] And the things that you have heard from me among many witnesses, commit these to faithful men who will be able to teach others also. [3] You therefore must endure hardship as a good soldier of Jesus Christ. [4] No one engaged in warfare entangles himself with the affairs of *this* life, that he may please him who enlisted him as a soldier. [5] And also if anyone competes in athletics, he is not crowned unless he competes according to the rules.

It seems that the formation of the New Testament church, built upon the ministry of the apostles and prophets, had their governmental structure built up within it from the inside out. Jesus laid the foundation of democracy when He stated that the highest authority in discipline was the local church assembled:

> Matthew 18:17 (NKJV)
> [17] And if he refuses to hear them, tell *it* to the church. But if he refuses even to hear the church, let him be to you like a heathen and a tax collector.

We read in the book of Acts how different individuals were led to the Lord to preach the Gospel, and people were born again. People simply released the gifts, and ministries flowed out of them. If they taught and were anointed, they were considered teachers. Prophets were recognized informally. When a problem arose, the church sent representatives to deal with it:

> Acts 15:2-3 (NKJV)
> [2] Therefore, when Paul and Barnabas had no small dissension and dispute with them, they determined that Paul and Barnabas and certain others of them should go up to Jerusalem, to the apostles and elders, about this question. [3] So, being sent on their way by the church, they passed through Phoenicia and Samaria, describing the conversion of the Gentiles; and they caused great joy to all the brethren.

The church sent the representatives to those recognized as leaders (simply those who first heard the revelation of the Gospel and spread it). These representatives became local leaders and elders, representing the people. We know this since churches existed for almost two years before actual ordination of elders took place. Certainly there were leaders present, not formally recognized. However, to this representative type of government trans-local ministry would be added to serve in the spirit of the old senate of Israel.

Acts 13:1-3 (NKJV)
¹ Now in the church that was at Antioch there were certain prophets and teachers: Barnabas, Simeon who was called Niger, Lucius of Cyrene, Manaen who had been brought up with Herod the tetrarch, and Saul. ² As they ministered to the Lord and fasted, the Holy Spirit said, "Now separate to Me Barnabas and Saul for the work to which I have called them." ³ Then, having fasted and prayed, and laid hands on them, they sent *them* away.

Here trans-local ministry was born by the Spirit of God and the agreement of the local, elected leadership. Once again, just like the Old Testament, those already recognized became candidates for trans-local ministry representing the whole church, local and universal. This balanced out the representation of local needs (like the response of electing deacons in Acts 6) with the representation of principle and vision of the church as a whole.

Revelation 2:1 (NKJV)
¹ "To the angel of the church of Ephesus write ..."

As time progressed, it is obvious from Scripture that plural elder leadership was evident in the local churches. These elders included both local and trans-local, those elected and those sent out, and were recognized by the present leadership. Paul, the apostle, was one of these kinds of leaders. However, it became apparent that someone must take the lead, and the element of the one was added at some point. By the time the Book of Revelation was completed, there were individuals who represented local churches (most commentators see this as the best explanation of the word *angel* which means "messenger"). Thus, the one, few and many elements are seen in the early church as well.

Thus, the local church in the New Testament was composed of a simple government. The elders represented the operation of the one (senior elder), few (trans-local elders), and many (representative elders) in governing the local church. The deacons represented the service needs in the ministry of helps within the local church and governed in this area. In keeping with God's principle of sovereignty, the elders and deacon board form two decentralized areas of jurisdiction, though working together in the same vision and philosophy. A hierarchy or pyramid of running all things through the elders only stifles the flow and freedom of ministry within the local church.

We must remember that the purpose of leadership in the body of Christ is to equip the saints of God to do the ministry, not keep the saints of God dependent upon the ministry from key leaders. The common belief all too often today is that God's authority and power flow directly to the leaders and then to the body of Christ. Thus, those in the church rule by "divine right" rather than voluntary consent of the governed. This leads to abuse of power, and the body of Christ becomes merely dependent upon officers for revelation, direction, protection, and provision rather than Christ Himself.

Although this is often stated, we need to practice the flow of power that will best bring this vision to pass. If we adopt a power flow that is not different, then we are pre-reformation in our thinking and in need of spiritual revolution, since we feel that God's power flows from Him to the leaders and then to us. If we do not reverse this idea and concept, we will continue to repeat the mistakes of the past and provide no adequate model for society to follow.

What can we learn from this? Whenever you have people, you have function. Whenever you have function, you have form. In other words, "form" and "structure" are inevitable. You cannot have "organism" without "organization". Whenever you attempt to achieve a goal or apply a principle, you must develop a procedure or pattern for doing it. You cannot communicate a "message" without a "method". You cannot teach "truth" without developing some form of "tradition".

The local church or community organization is no exception. Whenever you have people actively functioning in various roles, you have form and structure. Note that it is not possible to describe function without describing form.

The Bible often teaches function without describing form. Where it does describe form, it is partial and incomplete. What form is described varies from situation to situation. Functions and principles can be seen as absolute, but form is not. Social historians have made two important observations: in studying people and their societal structures, they have discovered that over a period of time, people tend to fixate particularly on forms. People resist change. Studies show there is one constant in history: that constant is fixity. Social studies also point out that people change their form and structures in society, basically under one condition – some kind of crisis. Then, and only then, are people open to change.

Christians differ little from people in general. Structure provides a sense of security. When we tamper with societal structures, we are tampering with people's emotional stability. This causes anxiety, and anxiety causes defensive reactions that always result in resistance to change. As Christians, sometimes we come under double trouble. Because we believe there are things that should never change, we often confuse non-absolutes (those things that should change) with absolutes (those things that should not change). Often this resistance is rooted in insecurity and fear and leads to rationalization.

Some people simple resist change because they are confused. They don't understand the difference between absolutes and non-absolutes. They think the prayer at the beginning of service is in the same category as the virgin birth. It is important for us to know the difference between: absolutes and non-absolutes; functions and forms; principles and patterns; truth and tradition; organism and organization; message and method; that which is supracultural and that which is purely cultural.

We have a God-given means to bring about crisis in the lives of Christians that can bring significant change. I'm speaking of the Word of God. Wherever and whenever God's truth is taught, it should create a spirit directed crisis in the life of every believer who is out of harmony with that truth. If we are to be in the will of God, we must change our attitudes and behavior and conform our lives to God's Word. If we yearn for reformation, we must live in the creative tension between order and renewal, between form and reformation. In our openness to receive God's new wine, at times we will discard old wineskins, but we will need new wineskins to replace them.

Discussion Questions

1. What signs of community maturation are seen in this chapter?
2. Discuss the importance of having a balanced governmental structure?
3. What is the purpose of leadership in the Body of Christ?
4. How might leadership be encouraged and multiplied?

CHAPTER 12
JOYFUL CELEBRATION

There is an exuberant joy that we feel after finishing a long project. Examples of these are: completing a college degree, building or remodeling a new home, or watching your children grow and get married. The text of Nehemiah does not say that when the wall was finished (Neh. 6:15) that there was any celebration or dedication. The flow in the narrative continued for several chapters as an indication that the wall was not an end in itself, but only a means to the end of a renewed covenant people.

Chapters 8-10 form the emotional apex of Ezra-Nehemiah as both leaders work together to usher in a new era of covenantal commitment. Finally in Chapter 13, we read of the joyous celebration. The people of Judah dedicated the wall with pageantry. In fact, their ceremony would compete for dramatic impact with any Harvard graduation, presidential inauguration, or holiday parade.

Preparation for Celebration (Nehemiah 12:27-30)

In preparation for the dedication, "The Levites" were gathered from their places of residence. Not only did they assist the priests, but the Levites also provided the music in the temple. Special "singers", who may or may not have been Levites, also gathered in Jerusalem from the surrounding villages (v. 28-29).

Once the appropriate personnel had arrived, "the priests and the Levites purified themselves, and purified the people, the gates, and the walls" (v. 30). Religious purification in the Old Testament took various forms, including washings, ritual sprinkling, sacrifices, fasting, and sexual abstinence. The priests and Levites participated in one or more of these means of ritual purification. Even the gates and the walls were purified, though the text does not explain how.

Preparation for the dedication involved gathering the participants and directing them to prepare themselves through rites of purification. The description of verses (31-43) reflects the careful design and implementation of the planned pageant, parades, choirs, and sacrifices.

Dedication of the Wall (Nehemiah 12:31-43)

The Jews were accustomed to having workers and watchers on the walls of Jerusalem, but now Nehemiah and Ezra assigned people to be worshippers on the walls. They conducted a dedication service with such enthusiasm that their shouts and songs were heard even afar off (v. 43).

The people had been dedicated (Neh. 8-10); now it was time to dedicate the work that the people had done. This is the correct order, for what good are dedicated walls and gates without dedicated people? Note the emphasis was on *joyful praise* on the part of the people. *Singing* is mentioned eight times in this chapter, *thanksgiving* six times, *rejoicing* seven times, and musical instruments three times.

To begin the dedication, Nehemiah divided the people into two groups. Each group contained: a large thanksgiving choir (Neh. 12:31), a significant lay leader (Hoshaiah, 12:32; Nehemiah, 12:38), other leaders (12:32-34,40), priests with trumpets (12:35-36, 41) and other musicians, including the Levites (12:36, 42).

From the point where they had gathered, Nehemiah sent one group counter-clockwise along the top of the wall, and he directed another group in a clockwise direction. After walking around on most of the wall, both groups converged at the temple (v. 40). Along the way, I'm sure that everyone had memories of what they participated in building. There, while the singers sang loudly with Jezrahiah as their director (v. 42), the priest offered great sacrifices

(v. 43). All the people rejoiced with great joy including the women and the children (v. 43

Why did Ezra and Nehemiah organize this dedication service? Why not just meet at the temple area, let the Levites sing and offer sacrifices to the Lord, and send everybody home? To begin with, it was the walls and gates that were being dedicated, and it was only right that the people see and touch them. But there is another reason for this unique service: the people were bearing witness to the watching world that God had done the work, and He alone should be glorified. The enemy had said that the walls would be so weak that a fox could knock them down (Neh. 4:3), but here were the people marching on the walls! What a testimony to the unbelieving Gentiles of the power and reality of faith. It was another opportunity to prove to them that this work was wrought by God (Neh. 6:16).

By marching on the walls, the people had an opportunity to see the results of their labors and realize anew that one person had not done the work. True, Nehemiah had been their leader, and they needed him, but the people had a mind to work (Neh. 4:6). Various people and families had labored on different parts of the wall (Neh. 3), but nobody owned the part he or she had worked on. The wall belonged to God.

Marching around these walls was a symbolic act by which the Jews stepped out in faith to claim God's blessing. In that day, to walk on a piece of property meant to claim it as your own. God said to Abraham, "Arise, walk through the land ... for I will give it unto thee (Gen. 13:17", and He said to Joshua, "Every place that the sole of your foot shall tread upon, that have I given unto you" (Josh. 1:3). This joyful march around the walls was their way of saying, "We claim from our God all that He has for us, just as our forefathers claimed this land by faith!"

Too often a church dedication service marks the end and not the beginning of ministry as the congregation breathes a sigh of relief and settles down to business as usual. If we lose our forward vision and stop launching out by faith, then what God has accomplished will become a millstone rather than a milestone that will burden and break us.

But the most important thing about this dedication service was not the march around the walls. It was the expression of joyful praise that came from the choirs and the people (Heb. 13:15; Psalm 69:30-31).

The people offered their praise thankfully (Neh. 12:24, 27, 31, 38, 46), joyfully (v. 27, 43-44), and loudly (v. 42-43), accompanied by various instruments (v. 27, 35-36). It was not a time for muted meditative worship. It was time for pulling out all the stops and praising the Lord enthusiastically.

It was not only the professional musicians who expressed praise to God, for the women and children also joined in the singing (Neh. 12:43). They had heard the Word at the Water Gate (Neh. 8:2), so it was only right that they now express their worship, for learning the Word and worshiping the Lord must go together (Col. 3:1-2). We must never permit the accomplished ministry of worship leaders to take the place of our own spontaneous celebration of the Lord's goodness. Otherwise, we will become spectators instead of participants; and spectators miss most of the blessing.

Effective Worship - Nehemiah 12:27-43

The people of God dedicated the wall in Jerusalem with an elaborate worship service. This suggests how we might worship God more fully. As the Israelites celebrated God's provision of a wall, so we gather as Christians to celebrate God's grace offered through Christ. As they dedicated the wall, so we dedicate ourselves in worship.

Nehemiah 12:27-43 offers four aspects of effective worship: pausing, preparation, participation, and physical expression.

Pausing to Celebrate

The people of Judah paused to dedicate the wall. The Levites from a wide area took time away from their appointed duties to celebrate this event. All of the people including religious and secular leaders – stepped back from their daily tasks in order to celebrate. The text does not indicate exactly how long the dedication lasted, but it must have lasted at least a day, and for many the preparations probably required much more time.

When we gather for worship, we also pause, stepping back from our typically busy lives to focus on God. Sadly, the notion of pausing for anything has become increasingly foreign to our culture. We fill our lives with endless activities, rushing through them at a frenetic pace. It's not surprising that worship often gets lost in the shuffle.

But God created us to pause. He created us to live in a steady rhythm in which we rest from our labors one day each week. The Sabbath was created for us that we might pause for refreshment, for rest, and for worship. You and I must build into our lives time to pause, to enjoy God and to enjoy life.

It's not easy for some of us to pause. As soon as one project is over my pragmatism presses me forward onto the next one. Consequently, too often I miss the joy along the way. It's like taking a trip. The wife says what she saw along the way. The husband says how fast he got there. So much of life passes us by. When we are young, we want to be a teenager. When we are teenagers we want to drive, etc. We are never happy with the present state. Our life is not enriched when we let our work ethic take command of our life. We never have enough – we always want more. Likewise, as we consider our relationship with God, we need to take time to pause, reflect, pray and to celebrate with others.

Preparation for Worship

The priests and Levites prepared for their service by purifying themselves. We do not know what physical action this entailed. It provided these religious leaders with a chance to prepare their hearts for serving God. If they wash their clothes, for example, focusing on physical cleanliness gave them the opportunity to consider their spiritual readiness for worship.

Unfortunately, many Christians do not prepare themselves for worship. Do we set aside time to prepare our hearts to bow in the presence of God? Perhaps we need to begin on Saturday evening, setting aside a time for reflection and prayer. Before going to church on Sunday mornings, you may spend time listening to Christian music, writing in your journal, praying – preparing your heart and mind for worship. But as I watch our members arriving in a rush, often trailing children after them, I realize that times of quiet are few and far between for many of them. That's why maintaining an attitude of worship with pre-service prayer is so important. During this time, we prepare to worship by quieting our spirits, reflecting on God, and allowing the Holy Spirit to move in our hearts.

Participating in Worship

The people of Israel did not dedicate the walls by sitting and listening; they participated by processing (v. 38) and by rejoicing (v. 43). The Levites and other music directors led them in song. As a result of their active participation, the singing was heard from far away.

Worship is not something we observe; it is something we do. Worship is a performance in which God is the audience and the congregants are the performers. Those who lead worship are only prompters, not performers to be observed by the congregation.

Many Christians miss this point. They attend worship every Sunday in order to watch the show, to get something out of the sermon, to be inspired, and return home. These reasons may be worthy, but they are not worship. True worship occurs when we communicate with God, when we offer our praise, our love, and our very lives to Him.

As a pastor, I am concerned with how easily we fall into an observational mode in church. The arrangements of church services often encourage this mode. The pastor speaks from the front. The worship leaders lead from the front. Like actors on a stage, the action from the platform makes a congregation believe they are the audience. The truth is that you are the performers; God is the audience; and the leaders are simply the prompters.

Physical Expression in Worship

In their service of dedication, the Israelites marched around the city walls. They sang and rejoiced with such gusto that neighbors from miles around heard the noise; they were involved physically as well as mentally and spiritually. The Old Testament abounds with physical expressions of worship. People sing, shout, kneel, bow, clap their hands, raise their hands, and dance. In fact, rarely do we read that they simply sit. In a Biblical view, God sits enthroned while worshippers kneel or stand before Him as a gesture of submission and servitude.

In some Christian traditions, the physical expression of worship is minimized. Singing is done quietly. The confession of faith is done with reverent reservation. Emphasis is placed on the intellectual component of true worship with slight allowance for the emotional and with great restraint.

Certainly, true worship involves the mind, for we think about God and communicate cognitively with Him in worship. But perhaps we need to learn more about loving God with all of our heart, and all of our soul, and all of our strength (Deut. 6:5).

Singing, one of the physical expressions of worship, is central to Biblical worship. The dedication in Nehemiah 12 illustrates this principle distinctly. Ten of the seventeen verses in Nehemiah 12:27-43 mention something musical. Levites came from miles around to play their instruments and sing in the choir. The people participated by singing with great joy and with great volume.

If we turn to the Psalms, we find that they reiterate the fundamental role of singing in worship (Psalm 91, 95, 96, 98, 100).

All of this brings to mind the words of Martin Luther, who was effusive in his praise of music:

> *"I wish to see all arts, principally music, in the service of Him who gave and created them. Music is a fair and glorious gift of God. I would not for the world forego my humble share of music. Singers are never sorrowful, but are merry, and smile through their troubles in song. Music makes people kinder, gentler, more staid and reasonable. I am strongly persuaded that after theology there is no art that can be placed on a level with music; for besides theology, music is the only art capable of affording peace and joy of the heart ... the devil flees before the sound of music almost as much as before the Word of God."*

Perhaps more than any other medium, music and singing unites our hearts, souls, minds and bodies. Of course, mere physical expression of worship that does not emanate from the heart does not honor God. On the other hand, our bodies can influence our hearts to genuinely experience worship. When I kneel in prayer, I often find my heart unexpectedly humbled before God.

I can imagine that, as the people of Israel walked upon the wall, they had finished by God's grace; heartfelt thanksgiving began to well up inside of them. As they sang loud praises, surely their hearts filled with even more joy.

Wouldn't our worship be enriched if we began to follow Psalm 95 literally?

> Psalm 95:1-7 (NKJV)
> [1] Oh come, let us sing to the LORD! Let us shout joyfully to the Rock of our salvation. [2] Let us come before His presence with thanksgiving; Let us shout joyfully to Him with psalms. [3] For the LORD *is* the great God, And the great King above all gods. [4] In His hand *are* the deep places of the earth; The heights of the hills *are* His also. [5] The sea *is* His, for He made it; And His hands formed the dry *land.* [6] Oh come, let

us worship and bow down; Let us kneel before the LORD our Maker. ⁷ For He *is* our God, And we *are* the people of His pasture, And the sheep of His hand. Today, if you will hear His voice:

Discussion Questions

1. Why is it important to prepare for celebration?
2. Why must you dedicate what we build?
3. What four aspects of effective worship did Nehemiah offer?
4. Why is it important to recognize normal work and rest cycles in your life?
5. How does worship involve the whole person?
6. Consider how you have made celebration a part of your life? How might you implement it in a more meaningful way?

CHAPTER 13
LIFELONG SERVANT LEADERSHIP

A Day of Obedience – Nehemiah 12:44-13:3

This short passage serves as a transition between the climatic dedication in Nehemiah 12:27-43 and the later work of Nehemiah 13:4-31. It summarizes the covenant life of Israel after the wall had been built, while it presents the issues to be considered in the rest of Chapter 13.

"On that day" gives the impression of activities that occurred on the same day in which the wall had been dedicated, but verse 47 shows the editor's broader intention: "In the days of Zerubbabel and in the days of Nehemiah." This passage describes a time that begins with the dedication but continues for an unspecified period of time. In ancient times, persons were appointed to supervise the storehouse of tithes for those who served in the Temple (v. 44). They also gathered these tithes "from the fields of the cities (v. 44). Here it appears that the people were more than willing to offer the required portions, since "Judah rejoiced over the priests and Levites who ministered" (v. 44). Under the influence of Nehemiah, the people ordered their life according to God's covenant and even took joy in the sacred institutions.

The results of this joyful service of dedication were a plentiful supply of produce to sustain the work of the ministry. The people gave not grudgingly or of necessity, but joyfully and gratefully (2 Cor. 9:7). Our material gifts are really spiritual sacrifices to the Lord, if they are given in the right spirit. The

Apostle Paul called the gifts from the Philippians' church an odor of a sweet smell, a sacrifice acceptable, well pleasing to God (Phil. 4:18). Jesus accepted Mary's gift of precious ointment as an act of worship, and Hebrews 13:16 reminds us that doing good and sharing are sacrifices that please the Lord.

When David established the order for Priest and Levites (1 Chr. 23-24) he also formed divisions of musicians and gatekeepers (1 Chr. 25-26). By mentioning the singers and gatekeepers (v. 45-46), Nehemiah paints a picture of a Temple that was completely operational, one in which all ministries occurred as in the former days. The temple was fully staffed and all Israel supported the ministry by giving the required tithes and other portions (v. 47). Under Nehemiah's leadership, the Temple and the nation functioned according to covenantal stipulations.

Again, "on that day" means, "during that period of time." The leaders read a passage from Deuteronomy 23:3-6. Upon hearing this passage the Israelites "separated all the mixed multitude" from Israel (Neh. 13:3). We do not know exactly what they did in separating themselves; the important thing to see is that all Israel endeavored to obey God's Word. Sadly, as we shall see, this period did not last long. There is indication that all agreed to do this; in practical terms, few actually did.

Shoring Up Restoration Life:
Nehemiah's Second Term – Nehemiah 13:4-31

Unlike the fairy tales of old, Nehemiah does not conclude his writing with "and they lived happily ever after." Unlike the Hollywood approach to ending this story on the high note, Nehemiah ends his writing in a gloomy dose of realism. Returning as the narrator, Nehemiah tells us about his second term as governor of Judah (Neh. 13:4-31). This passage can be divided into three sections, each beginning with a temporal reference ("how before this") ("in those days") and ending with a prayer of remembrance ("remember me"). Each section describes one way in which the people had forsaken their covenantal vows, as well as Nehemiah's decisive response to their unfaithfulness. The theme of the chapter is "Holiness."

Restoring the Holiness of the Temple
Nehemiah 13:4-14

Before the Israelites separated from the mixed multitude, a priest named "Eliashib" had been given responsibility for the "storerooms" of the Temple. It is not clear whether he was an ally, or perhaps even a relative of Tobiah (the archrival of Nehemiah. 2:19; 4:3, 7; 6:1, 14, 17-19). But it is clear that he allowed Tobiah to use a large storeroom of the Temple, presumably to extend his business and political contacts in Jerusalem.

This reveals two discouraging factors. One, it indicates that the required offerings were not being given for the support of the Temple ministry, hence the empty storeroom. Secondly, Tobiah was a Gentile, an Ammonite (Neh. 2:19), who should not have been allowed in the sacred areas of the Temple. Tobiah's presence in the storeroom designated for holy implements caused the room to be desecrated. It is perplexing that this compromise of the Temple's holiness and integrity did not appear to matter to Eliashib or his fellow priests.

Meanwhile, Nehemiah had left Jerusalem and returned to King "Artaxerxes" (v. 6). His initial 12-year stay ended in the 32nd year of the King's reign (5:14). Nehemiah does not say how many years passed before, once again, he obtained "leave from the King" in order to return to Jerusalem. He does not mention being sent as governor, but his authoritative actions in Chapter 13 make this a likely possibility.

Nehemiah reacted with strong emotion; he was "bitterly grieved (v. 8). He not only felt strongly, but he acted decisively. He threw "all the household goods of Tobiah out of the room" and commanded that the "rooms" be cleaned. Nehemiah was consumed with the same zeal for the Father's house as Jesus, who cleared the moneychangers' tables. Throughout this chapter, Nehemiah stands out from his contemporaries by his refusal to allow for a moment the idea that holiness is negotiable or that custom alone can hallow anything. Finally, Nehemiah restocked the storeroom with the "articles" and "offerings" originally intended to be stored there.

At this time, Nehemiah discovered that "the portions for the Levites had not been given them, for each of the Levites and the singers who did work had gone back to his field" (v. 10). Although not stated, the text seems to imply that the Levites and singers had left their ministry to provide for themselves because their support from the Temple had ceased. When the Temple was functioning properly, these ministers were supported fully by offerings given for their livelihood. When they were withheld, the Levites and singers could not continue with their sacred tasks. This explains why they had returned to their fields. A grudging attitude to tithes and offerings was a mark of the times. The temptation was to give as little as one could. Malachi expressed this as robbing God by default.

Nehemiah held the "rulers" (the civil officials) accountable for the failed support of the Levites and singers (v. 11). He contended with the leaders saying, "Why is the House of God forsaken?" Incredibly, the people had done precisely what they had promised not to do in the covenant of Chapter 10. They had pledged, "And we will not neglect the House of God" (Neh. 10:39). When Nehemiah accused the leaders of neglecting or forsaking the Temple, he was actually accusing them of breaking the covenant made in Chapter 10. Each incident in Chapter 13 follows this same pattern: the people break their covenantal vows from Chapter 10.

After contending with the leaders, Nehemiah reinstated the forsaken ministers in their proper places (v. 11). Under Nehemiah's command, "all Judah" once again brought the appropriate offerings to the storehouse and, thus, restored full support for the Temple staff. This time, however, he guaranteed that the guardians of the storehouse would be more "faithful" than the compromising Eliashib (v. 13). Nehemiah himself appointed the storehouse "treasurers", choosing people distinguished for their integrity.

This portion ends with the first of three prayers in which Nehemiah asks God to remember him. Additionally he asked, "Do not wipe out my good deeds that I have done for the house of my God, and for its services" (v. 14)! "Good deeds" is translated from the Hebrew word *"hesed"*, which means "my acts of faithfulness." This original word is often used of actions done in light of the covenant.

Nehemiah's actions were not simply "good deeds," but deeds done in covenant faithfulness to God. Nehemiah asked God not to "wipe out" his actions, perhaps reflecting the fact that his earlier deeds on behalf of the Temple had been wiped out – not by God, but by an unfaithful people and especially by their unfaithful leaders.

Restoring the Holiness of the Sabbath
Nehemiah 13:15-22

Nehemiah observed the people dishonoring the Sabbath. Immediately, he warned the transgressors not to sell goods on the Sabbath. The "men of Tyre" who lived in Jerusalem brought their goods into the city and sold them "to the children of Judah" (v. 16). As Gentiles, they did not follow the Sabbath Law, but by setting up shop on the Sabbath, they were corrupting the Judeans. Nehemiah did not rebuke the Tyrians but contended with the nobles of Judah.

Nehemiah warned the nobles that by profaning the Sabbath, they would bring "added wrath upon Israel." Not satisfied with his attempt to persuade the people, Nehemiah then commanded the gates of Jerusalem to be shut and to be guarded during the Sabbath so that no merchant could enter (v. 19). The sellers camped outside hoping to be able to sell goods to individuals who left the city during the Sabbath (v. 20). But when Nehemiah threatened these merchants with physical violence, they stopped coming to Jerusalem on the Sabbath (v. 21).

Finally, Nehemiah commanded the "Levites" to cleanse themselves" and "guard the gates" (v. 22). This was an unusual assignment for the Levites. The fact that the Levites were to cleanse themselves ritually for such a mundane task seems particularly odd. Yet it indicated the sacredness of the assignment in Nehemiah's view. By guarding the gates, the Levites would "sanctify the

Sabbath day." True holiness, according to Nehemiah pertains not only to what happens within the Temple precincts, but, equally, to life outside in the Holy City.

Once more the people broke covenant by buying and selling on the Sabbath when they had promised they would not (Neh. 10:31). Nehemiah exercised his authority to restore the sanctity of the Sabbath and to insure the ongoing faithfulness of the people. By locking the city gates and posting guards, he exposed his distrust of the people and their own convictions.

The prayer of remembrance that concludes this section evinces a spirit of resignation rather than of hope. Not only did Nehemiah seek God's recollection of his effort to sanctify the Sabbath, but also he asked God, "Spare me according to the greatness of Your mercy" (v. 22)! Perhaps Nehemiah foresaw the potential for Israel's destruction once again with the people's disobedience, not only to the 10 commandments, but also to their own specific promises. He was asking to be spared, not because of his own faithfulness but because of God's great mercy!

Restoring the Holiness of the People
Nehemiah 13:23-31

Nehemiah observes yet another instance of covenant breaking: some people of Judah "had married women of Ashdod, Ammon, and Moab." Verse 24 indicated that intermarriage with Ashdodites was the chief issue here since Nehemiah observed that children with Ashdodites mothers "could not speak the language of Judah." In response, Nehemiah not only confronted those who had intermarried, he hit them, pulled out their hair, and forced them to swear that they would not marry non-Jews. He made them repeat their covenantal promise. Nehemiah's exaggerated reaction may seem rash to modern readers. His actions of not only confronting, but also of hitting and pulling hair seem to be violent over-reactions.

Why did Nehemiah feel so strongly about mixed marriages? Intermarriage threatened the religious integrity of Israel. It was a threat to the cultural survival of the Hebrew people for mixed marriages produced children who could not speak the traditional language – the chief conveyance of cultures. Nehemiah recognized the sinfulness of intermarriage and the tendency of pagan wives to lead their husbands into sin and false religions.

Nehemiah is concerned namely with the corruption of the next generation. The babble of language among the children was not only a symptom but also a threat. It meant steady erosion of Israelite identity at the level of all thinking and expression, and a loss of access to the Word of God, which would effectively paganize them. A single generation could undo the work of centuries.

The people so lightly regarded this issue that even the priest had intermarried. Verses 30-31 summarize Nehemiah's efforts to reestablish a state of holiness within Israel and to refurbish the ministry of priest and Levites. Nehemiah talks of what he accomplished without mentioning the support of the people. Although he compelled the people to bring proper offerings, to honor the Sabbath, and to abstain from mixed marriages, nowhere in the chapter do we see evidence of their enthusiasm for his labors. The fact that Nehemiah had to appoint treasurers (v. 13) and guards (v. 19-22) is surely an indication of the people's reticence to be reformed.

In his final prayer, Nehemiah asked simply: "Remember me, O my God, for good" (v. 31)! Nehemiah asked God to remember not his great and lasting successes but simply himself.

Reflections on Nehemiah 13:4-31

The story of Nehemiah ends not with a bang, but with a whimper. The era of sweeping restoration and widespread, popular enthusiasm had ended. Each promise made by the people in Chapter 10 was broken in Chapter 13. Although Nehemiah still had the power to enforce obedience, he moved the people to holiness in deed only, not in heart.

The conclusion of Ezra-Nehemiah reflects a sad yet compelling realism. Nehemiah told the truth – even when the truth hurt. Perhaps he told the story of restoration to foreshadow and explain the failure of restoration in his own day. The Bible tells it like it is. So do Biblically committed leaders. The more we tell the truth, the more we will earn a hearing in our churches and world.

What was Israel's problem? Why did the reforms of Ezra and Nehemiah fail, at least in part? In Nehemiah 13 we see God's people allowing the world to invade what should be holy, set apart for God alone. They fail to live holy lives with respect to the Temple. Foreign traders tempted the Jews to dishonor the Sabbath, and men of Judah married foreign wives, only to bear children who could not speak Hebrew. This was because the fathers refused to follow the instruction of Deuteronomy 6. They were not willing to train the next generation.

We, contemporary Christians, face similar pressures to compromise our holiness. In our efforts to be accepted by the world, we allow non-Biblical values to "live within the church". We want preachers to stop talking about sin because it is offensive to modern ears. The idea of keeping the Sabbath rarely enters our minds. We fill our lives to the brim, rushing from one thing to another, filling the Lord's Day with shopping, chores and extra hours in the office. Then we wonder why we are so exhausted and "stressed out". The Bible teaches us to honor marriage and keep the bed undefiled (Heb. 13:4). Marital infidelity seems commonplace today, even among Christians, not to mention Christian leaders.

Time and again, Israel allowed the world and its fallen idols to invade her life. In Paul's words, she became "conformed to this world" (Rom. 12:2). Surely, we need to hear once again Paul's cry to holy living.

> Romans 12:1-2 (NKJV)
> [1] I beseech you therefore, brethren, by the mercies of God, that you present your bodies a living sacrifice, holy, acceptable to God, *which is* your reasonable service. [2] And do not be conformed to this world, but be transformed by the renewing of your mind, that you may prove what *is* that good and acceptable and perfect will of God.

True transformation requires more than coerced holiness; it begins with an inner transformation that flows into tangible acts of faithfulness.

In Ezra and Nehemiah we have observed outstanding leadership. Both men moved a nation into a season of rebuilding and renewal, and both experienced measurable success in their efforts. Ezra taught the people to obey the law. Nehemiah led the people to rebuilding Jerusalem's fallen wall. Together, Ezra and Nehemiah oversaw a fundamental renewal of the covenant between God and His chosen nation.

But our delight in the success of our heroes stumbles over the dreary and dismal accounts of Chapter 13. A couple of decades after Ezra's victory over intermarriage, many Jews continued to marry pagan women. For all of Nehemiah's efforts to protect Jerusalem from the world by building a wall, pagan influences continued to invade and corrupt God's people. When righteous behavior occurred, it happened, not because a renewed people chose to act in covenant faithfulness, but only because Nehemiah still had the power to coerce their obedience. We would be inclined to say, that in the end, Ezra and Nehemiah failed as leaders. On that level they did – if we measure success by the pervasive and lasting transformation of Israel, then neither Ezra nor Nehemiah ultimately succeeded.

But we find with the prayers of Chapter 13 a different way to measure leadership. First, Nehemiah asked God to remember his deed of covenant faithfulness (v. 14). Later, he asked the Lord to spare him according to God's great mercy (v. 22). Finally, Nehemiah prayed for God to simply remember him – not his works, but himself with favor.

In the end, Nehemiah's success may be evaluated, not on the basis of walls completed or laws enforced, but in light of his faithfulness to God and God's covenant. Similarly, God weighs Nehemiah's efforts, not by how much or how little he accomplished, but in light of God's own faithful mercy.

To the end, Nehemiah tried to honor God and to lead in light of the covenant. He succeeded, not by persuading the nation to follow him, but by living and leading faithfully before God. And where he fell short, God's mercy compensated.

What matters most in the end is not Nehemiah's achievements, but his character and his relationship with God. What will matter in the end for all of us will not be so much what we did for God but our relationship with God and His character revealed through us. This will require that we remember the Lord's covenant with us and we allow Him to transform us.

In the end, the success of your ministry will not be how busy you can get, but do you know God and yield to His Lordship? A changed people will change communities.

Discussion Questions

1. Throughout the Bible are stories of successes and failures of God's people. What is the role of leadership called to do when there is little success or fruit seen in the lives of others?
2. What areas of prior covenantal renewal were let go by the people of Jerusalem?
3. Are these particular areas of importance to the modern church and the society around it? How so?
4. What lessons do you see in terms of having on going leadership influence in others lives?
5. What were some of the failures of leadership exposed in Chapter 13?
6. What important lessons can you apply to your life and ministry?
7. What have you learned that will make you a more effective leader?

Bibliography

Getz, Gene A. *Nehemiah: Becoming a Disciplined Leader*. Nashville, Tennessee: Broadman & Holman, 1995.

Kidner, Derek. *Tyndale Old Testament Commentaries: Ezra & Nehemiah*. Downers Grove, Illinois: Inter-varsity Press, 1979.

Linthicum, Robert C. *City of God City of Satan: A Biblical Theology of the Urban Church*. Grand Rapids, Michigan: Zondervan Publishing House, 1991.

Packer, J. I. *A Passion for Faithfulness: Wisdom from the Book of Nehemiah*. Wheaton, Illinois: Crossway Books, 1995.

Roberts, Mark D. *The Communicator's Commentary: Ezra, Nehemiah, Ester*. Dallas, Texas: Word Books, 1993.

Wiersbe, W. W. *Be Determined*. Wheaton Illinois: Victor Books, 1992.

www.ingramcontent.com/pod-product-compliance
Lightning Source LLC
LaVergne TN
LVHW011425080426
835512LV00005B/262